Saving Beauty

Byung-Chul Han

Saving Beauty

Translated by Daniel Steuer

polity

First published in German as *Die Errettung des Schönen* © S. Fischer Verlag GmbH, Frankfurt am Main, 2015

This English edition © Polity Press, 2018

Polity Press
65 Bridge Street
Cambridge CB2 1UR, UK

Polity Press
101 Station Landing, Suite 300,
Medford, MA 02155, USA

Extracts on pages vi and 77 from *Paul Celan: Selected Poems*, Author: Paul Celan, translated by: Michael Hamburger, © 1972. Reproduced with the kind permission of Johnson & Alcock Ltd.

ISBN-13: 978-1-5095-1509-7
ISBN-13: 978-1-5095-1510-3 (pb)

A catalogue record for this book is available from the British Library.

Library of Congress Cataloging-in-Publication Data
Names: Han, Byung-Chul, author.
Title: Saving beauty / Byung-Chul Han.
Description: English edition. | Cambridge, UK; Malden, MA:
Polity Press, [2017] | Includes bibliographical references and index.
Identifiers: LCCN 2017009266 (print) | LCCN 2017030526 (ebook) |
ISBN 9781509515127 (Mobi) | ISBN 9781509515134 (Epub) |
ISBN 9781509515097 | ISBN 9781509515103 (pb)
Subjects: LCSH: Aesthetics.
Classification: LCC BH39 (ebook) | LCC BH39 .H36 2017 (print) |
DDC 111/.85--dc23
LC record available at https://lccn.loc/gov/2017009266

Typeset in 11.5 on 15 pt Janson Text by
Servis Filmsetting Limited, Stockport, Cheshire
Printed and bound in Great Britain by Clays Ltd, St Ives PLC

For further information on Polity, visit our website:
politybooks.com

Contents

Once,
I heard him,
he was washing the world
unseen, nightlong,
real.

One and Infinite,
annihilated
ied.

Light was. Salvation.

Paul Celan[1]

1

The Smooth

The smooth is the signature of the present time. It connects the sculptures of Jeff Koons, iPhones and Brazilian
waxing. Why do we today find what is smooth beautiful? Beyond its aesthetic effect, it reflects a general social
imperative. It embodies today's *society of positivity*. What is
smooth does not *injure*. Nor does it offer any resistance. It
is looking for *Like*. The smooth object deletes its *Against*.
Any form of negativity is removed.

The aesthetics of the smooth is also adopted by
smartphones. The LG *G Flex* is even covered with a self-
healing skin which makes any scratch, that is, any trace
of an injury, disappear within the shortest of times. It
is invulnerable, so to speak. The artificial skin of this
smartphone keeps it smooth at all times. It is also flexible
and bendable, with a slight curvature so as to perfectly
follow the contours of the face and back pocket. This

1

adaptability and absence of resistance are essential characteristics of the aesthetics of the smooth.

Smoothness is not limited to the outside of the digital apparatus. Communication via a digital apparatus also appears smoothed out, as it is mostly polite remarks, even positivities, which are exchanged. 'Sharing' and 'Like' represent communicative means for smoothening. Negativities are eliminated because they represent obstacles to accelerated communication.

Jeff Koons, arguably the most successful living artist at present, is a master of smooth surfaces. Andy Warhol also professed his commitment to beautiful, smooth surfaces, but his art still had the negativity of death and disaster inscribed into it. His surfaces are not entirely smooth. The series *Death and Disaster*, for instance, still lives off negativity. In Jeff Koons's work, by contrast, there exists no disaster, no injury, no ruptures, also no seams. Everything flows in soft and smooth transitions. Everything appears rounded, polished, smoothed out. Jeff Koons's art is dedicated to smooth surfaces and their immediate effect. It does not ask to be interpreted, to be deciphered or to be reflected upon. It is an art in the age of *Like*.

Jeff Koons says that an observer of his works should only emit a simple 'Wow'. It seems that his art does not require any judgement, interpretation or hermeneutics, no reflection or thought. It intentionally remains infantile, banal, imperturbably relaxed, disarming and disburdening. It has been emptied of any depth, any shallows, any profound sense. Thus, his motto is: 'to take the observer into your arms'. Nothing is meant to shake, injure or shock the observer. Art, according to Jeff Koons, is nothing but 'beauty', 'joy' and 'communication'.

His smooth sculptures cause a 'haptic compulsion' to touch them, even the desire to suck them. His art lacks a negativity that would demand distance. It is the positivity of smoothness alone that causes the haptic compulsion. It invites the observer to take an attitude without distance, to *touch*. An *aesthetic* judgement, however, presupposes a *contemplative distance*. The art of the smooth abolishes such distance.

Haptic compulsion and the desire to suck can only arise in an art of the smooth that is devoid of meaning. Hegel, who emphatically held on to the arts being meaningful, therefore limited the sensual in the arts to 'the two theoretical senses of sight and hearing'.[1] They alone have access to meaning, while smell and taste are excluded from the enjoyment of art. The latter are only susceptible to the 'agreeable' which is not 'the beauty of art':[2] 'For smell, taste, and touch have to do with matter as such and its immediately sensible qualities – smell with material volatility in air, taste with the material liquefaction of objects, touch with warmth, cold, smoothness, etc.'[3] The smooth only conveys an agreeable feeling, which cannot be connected with any meaning or profound sense. It exhausts itself in a 'Wow'.

In his *Mythologies*, Roland Barthes points out the haptic compulsion which is triggered by the new Citroën *D.S.*:

> It is well known that smoothness is always an attribute of perfection because its opposite reveals a technical and typically human operation of assembling: Christ's robe was seamless, just as the airships of science-fiction are made of unbroken metal. The *D.S.* 19 has no pretensions about being as smooth as cake-icing, although its

3

general shape is very rounded; yet it is the dove-tailing of its sections which interest the public most: one keenly fingers the edges of the windows, one feels along the wide rubber grooves which link the back window to its metal surround. There are in the *D.S.* the beginnings of a new phenomenology of assembling, as if one progressed from a world where elements are welded to a world where they are juxtaposed and hold together by sole virtue of their wondrous shape, which of course is meant to prepare one for the idea of a more benign Nature.

As for the material itself, it is certain that it promotes a taste for lightness in its magical sense. . . . Here, the glass surfaces are not windows, openings pierced in a dark shell; they are vast walls of air and space, with the curvature, the spread and the brilliance of soap bubbles, . . .[4]

Jeff Koons's seamless sculptures also look like brilliant, weightless soap bubbles made of air and emptiness. Like the seamless *D.S.*, they confer a feeling of perfection, of lightness in a magical sense. They embody a perfect and optimized surface without depth and shallows.

For Roland Barthes, the sense of touch 'is the most demystifying of all senses, unlike sight which is the most magical'.[5] The sense of sight keeps a distance, while the sense of touch destroys it. Without distance, there can be no mysticism. De-mystification lets everything become available for enjoyment and consumption. The sense of touch destroys the negativity of what is wholly other. It secularizes what it touches. In contrast to the sense of sight, touch is incapable of wonderment. The smooth

4

touchscreen, therefore, is a place of de-mystification and total consumption. It produces what one *likes*.

Jeff Koons's sculptures are as *smooth as a mirror*, so to speak, allowing the observer to see him- or herself mirrored in them. On the occasion of the exhibition at the Beyeler Foundation, he remarked on his *Balloon Dog*:

> *The Balloon Dog* is really a wonderful object. It wants to confirm the observer in their existence. I often work with reflecting, mirroring materials because they automatically raise the self-confidence of the viewer. Of course, in a dark room that doesn't work. But if you stand right in front of the object, you are reflected in it and assured of yourself.[6]

The Balloon Dog is not a Trojan horse, it does not *hide* anything. There is no *inwardness* hidden behind its smooth surface.

As in the case of the smartphone, you only encounter yourself, and not the *other*, when faced with the highly polished sculptures. The motto of Koons's art: 'The core is always the same: learn to trust yourself and your own history. That is also what I want to convey to the observer of my work. The observer is meant to feel their own love of life.'[7] Art opens up an echo chamber, in which I assure myself of my own existence. The *alterity* or *negativity* of the *other* and the *alien* is eliminated altogether.

Jeff Koons's art possesses a *soteriological* dimension. It promises *salvation*. The world of smoothness is a culinary world, a world of pure positivity, in which there is no pain, no injury and no guilt. The *Balloon Venus* sculpture, shaped in birth position, is Jeff Koons's Holy

5

Mary. Yet, she does not give birth to a saviour, a *homo doloris* with a crown of thorns whose body is covered by wounds, but to champagne, a bottle of Dom Pérignon Rosé Vintage 2003, which is inside her belly. Jeff Koons presents himself as a Baptist promising salvation. It is no coincidence that there is a sequence of images from 1987 titled *Baptism*. Jeff Koons's art practises a *sacralization of the smooth*. He stages a *religion of the smooth, the banal*, even a *religion of consumption*. In their service, all negativity is to be eliminated.

For Gadamer, negativity is essential to art. It is its *wound*. It is opposed to the positivity of the smooth. There is *something* there which shakes me, an inner turmoil, which questions me and appeals to me: *You must change your life*:

> It is the fact that a particular thing such as this exists that constitutes the 'additional something'. As Rilke says 'Such a thing stood among men.' This fact that it exists, its facticity, represents an unsurmountable resistance against any superior presumption that we can make sense of it all. The work of art compels us to recognize this fact. 'There is no place that fails to see you. You must change your life.'[8]

A push comes from the work of art. It pushes the observer down. The smooth has an altogether different intentional nature. It adapts to the observer, elicits a *Like* from him or her. All it wants is to please, and not to knock over.

Today, the beautiful itself is smoothened out by taking any negativity, any form of shock or injury, out of it. The beautiful is exhausted in a *Like-it*. Aestheticization turns out to be anaestheticization; it sedates our perception.[9] Thus, Jeff Koons's 'wow' is also an anaesthetic reaction that is diametrically opposed to the negative experience of shock, of being knocked over. Today, the *experience* of beauty is impossible. Where the wish to please, the *Like*, edges its way into the foreground, *experience*, which is impossible without negativity, withers.

Smooth visual communication takes place in the form of *contagion*, without any aesthetic distance. The unbroken visibility of the object at the same time destroys the gaze. Only the rhythmic oscillation between presence and absence, veiling and unveiling, keeps the gaze awake. The erotic also depends on 'the staging of an appearance-as-disappearance',[10] on the 'undulations of the imaginary'.[11] The pornographic uninterrupted presence of the visible destroys the imaginary. Paradoxically, it presents *nothing to see*.

Today, not only the beautiful but also the ugly becomes smooth. The ugly also loses the negativity of the diabolical, of the uncanny and terrifying, and is smoothened out, a formula for consumption and enjoyment. It lacks entirely the fear- and terror-inducing gaze of the Medusa which petrifies everything. The ugly that was used by the artists and poets of the *fin de siècle* possessed something abysmal and demonic. The surrealist politics of the ugly served the purpose of provocation and emancipation; it marked a radical break from inherited patterns of perception.

Bataille saw in the ugly possibilities for overcoming boundaries and for liberation. For him, it offers access to transcendence:

7

No-one doubts the ugliness of the sexual act. Just as
death does in sacrifice, the ugliness of the sexual union
makes for anguish. But the greater the anguish . . . the
stronger the realisation of exceeding the bounds and the
greater the accompanying rush of joy.[12]

The essence of sexuality, according to this, is excess and
transgression. It delimits consciousness. This is what
constitutes its negativity.

Today, the entertainment industry exploits the ugly and
disgusting, making it consumable. Disgust is originally a
'state of alarm and emergency, an acute crisis of self-
preservation in the face of an unassimilable otherness, a
convulsive struggle, in which what is in question is, quite
literally, whether "to be or not to be"'.[13] The disgusting
is the non-consumable par excellence. The disgusting has
an existential dimension also for Rosenkranz. It is the
other of life, the other of form, *putrefaction*. A corpse
is a scandalous phenomenon because it still has a form,
although it is *in itself formless*. Due to the still existing
form, it retains the semblance of life, despite being dead:
'the negation of the beautiful form of an appearance
through a non-form originating in physical or moral
decay. . . . The appearance of life in what is dead in itself
is what is infinitely repulsive in disgust.'[14] The disgusting
as the infinitely repulsive evades any form of consumption. The disgusting which is today presented in the
'Dschungelcamp',[15] lacks any negativity that might trig-
ger an existential crisis. It is smoothened out into a form
for consumption.

Brazilian waxing makes the body *smooth*. It represents
today's compulsive hygiene. The essence of eroticism, for

8

Bataille, is soiling and, accordingly, compulsive hygiene would be its end. Dirty eroticism gives way to *clean pornography*. Depilated skin, in particular, gives the body a pornographic smoothness which is felt to be pure and clean. Today's society, obsessed with cleanliness and hygiene, is a society of positivity which feels disgust at any kind of negativity.

The hygienic compulsion takes hold of other areas as well. Everywhere, prohibitions are announced in the name of hygiene. Robert Pfaller is right when he says in his *Das schmutzige Heilige und die reine Vernunft* [The dirty sacred and pure reason]: 'If one tries to characterize by their common features those things which have, unnoticed, become impossible in our culture, one finds first of all that these things are often experienced as objects of disgust, as dirty.'[16]

From the perspective of hygienic reason, any ambivalence and any secret are also perceived to be dirty. Pure is transparency, and things become transparent when they fit into the smooth streams of information and data. Data have something pornographic and obscene about them. They have no inside, no *flip sides*; they are not *ambiguous*. In this, they differ from *language* which does not permit things to come into *perfectly clear focus*. Data and information deliver themselves to total visibility and they make everything visible.

Dataism introduces the second Enlightenment. Acts, which presuppose a free will, belong to the dogmas of the first Enlightenment. The second Enlightenment smoothens such acts into operations, into a *data-driven process* which takes place without any autonomy or dramatic orchestration of the subject. Acts become transparent

9

when they are operationalized, when they submit themselves to computable and controllable processes.

Information is a pornographic form of knowledge. It lacks the inwardness which characterizes knowledge. Knowledge also contains negativity in the sense that it is often *gained against a resistance*. Knowledge has an altogether different temporal structure from that of information. It stretches between past and future. Information, by contrast, dwells in a smoothened-out time that is made up of indifferent point-like presences. This is a time without events [*Ereignis*] and destiny.

The smooth is something one just likes. It lacks the negativity of *opposition*. It is no longer an *opposing body*. Today, communication also becomes smooth. It is smoothened out into a frictionless exchange of information. Smooth communication is free from any negativity of the other or alien. Communication reaches its maximum speed where like reacts to like. The resistance coming from the *other* disturbs the smooth communication of the same. The positivity of smoothness accelerates the circulation of information, communication and capital.

2

The Smooth Body

In contemporary films, the face is often shown in close-up. In a close-up, the whole body appears as pornographic. It divests the body of language. This muting of the body is pornographic. In a close-up, all its parts appear as if they were sexual organs: 'The close-up of a face is as obscene as a sexual organ looked at from a close distance. *It is* a sexual organ. Any picture, any form, any part of the body looked at from a close distance is a sexual organ.'[1]

For Walter Benjamin, the close-up was still a *linguistic, hermeneutic* practice. It *reads* the body. It makes the language of the unconscious legible behind the space informed by consciousness:

> With the close-up, space expands; with slow motion, movement is extended. And just as enlargement not merely clarifies what we see indistinctly 'in any case,'

but brings to light entirely new structures of matter, slow motion not only reveals familiar aspects of movements, but discloses quite unknown aspects within them ... Clearly, it is another nature which speaks to the camera as compared to the eye. 'Other' above all in the sense that a space informed by human consciousness gives way to a space informed by the unconscious. ... We are familiar with the movement of picking up a cigarette lighter or a spoon, but know almost nothing of what really goes on between hand and metal, and still less how this varies with different moods.[2]

In a close-up of the face, the background is altogether blurred. The close-up brings about a loss of world. The aesthetics of the close-up reflects a society which has become a close-up society itself. The face appears caught up in itself and becomes self-referential. It is no longer *world-containing*, which means that it is no longer *expressive*. A selfie is precisely such an empty, expressionless face. The addictive taking of selfies points towards the inner emptiness of the ego. The contemporary ego is very poor in stable forms of expressions with which it may identify, which would give it a solid identity. Today, nothing endures. This impermanence also affects the ego and de-stabilizes it, makes it insecure. And just this insecurity, this *anxiousness about oneself*, produces the addictive taking of selfies, produces a *self that is idling* and never comes to rest. Faced with its inner emptiness, the subject of the selfie tries in vain *to produce itself*. Selfie means *empty forms of the self*. It reproduces the emptiness. It is not a narcissistic self-love or vanity which generates the addictive taking of selfies, but an inner emptiness. There is no stable, narcissistic ego involved in this, which could love itself. Rather, we are dealing with a *negative narcissism*.

The close-up smoothens out the features [*Gesicht*] into a face [*Face*]. A face has neither depths nor shallows. It is just *smooth*. It lacks inwardness. Face means a façade (from Latin *facies*). The exhibition of the face as a façade does not require any depth of focus. Such a focus would even damage the façade. Thus, the shutter is fully open. An open shutter removes depth, the inwardness, the *gaze*. It makes the face appear obscene, pornographic. The intention of exhibiting destroys the *restraint* which constitutes the inwardness of the gaze: 'In fact, he is looking at nothing; he *retains* within himself his love and his fear: that is the Look.'[3] The face exhibiting itself is *without gaze*.

Today, the body is in crisis. It decomposes not only into pornographic body parts, but also into sets of digital data. The digital age is entirely dominated by the belief that life can be measured and quantified. The 'Quantified Self' movement also shares this creed.[4] The body is equipped with digital sensors which register all body-related data. 'Quantified Self' transforms the body into a control-and-surveillance screen. The collected data are also made available on the internet and exchanged. Dataism dissolves the body into data, makes it *data-compatible*. At the same time, it is dissected into partial objects which resemble sexual organs. The *transparent body* is no longer the *narrative* scene of the imagination. Rather, it is a sum of data or partial objects.

The digital network net-*works* the body. A self-driving car is nothing but a mobile information terminal to which I am merely *connected*. This makes driving a car a purely operational process. The speed is completely separated from the imagination. The car is no longer an extension of the body, charged with phantasmagorias of power, possession and appropriation. A self-driving car is no phallus. A phallus to which I am merely connected would be a contradiction. Car-sharing[5] is a profanation and disenchantment of the car. It also disenchants the body. The sharing principle does not apply to the phallus because the phallus is a symbol for possession, property and power as such. Categories of the sharing economy, such as connection or access, destroy the phantasmagorias of power and appropriation. In a self-driving car, I am not an actor, a demiurge or dramatic director; I am merely an *interface* within the global communication network.

3

The Aesthetics of the Smooth

The aesthetics of beauty is a genuine phenomenon of modern times. Only, in the aesthetics of modern times, the beautiful and the sublime become separated. The beautiful is isolated in its pure positivity. The subject of modern times, which becomes stronger and stronger, turns the beautiful into a positive object of pleasure. In this context, the beautiful is juxtaposed to the sublime, which – due to its negativity – does not cause immediate pleasure. The negativity of the sublime, which distinguishes it from the beautiful, is turned into something positive again when it is derived from human reason. At that point, it is no longer the *outside*, no longer the *wholly other*, but a form of *inner* expression of the subject.

In Pseudo-Longinus, who wrote the treatise *On the Sublime (peri hypsous)*, the beautiful and the sublime are not yet distinguished. Thus, part of the beautiful is the

15

negativity of the overwhelming. The beautiful by far exceeds the pleasurable. Beautiful women, according to Pseudo-Longinus, are 'tortures to the eyes'. Thus, they are *painfully beautiful*. Shocking and sublime beauty are not a contradiction. The negativity of pain deepens beauty. Here, the beautiful is anything but smooth.

Plato also does not distinguish between beauty and the sublime. The beautiful is unsurpassable precisely because it is sublime. In it inheres the negativity which is characteristic of the sublime. The sight of beauty does not cause pleasure, but shocks. At the end of the ascending ladder, the adept of beauty 'all of a sudden' catches sight of the 'wonderfully beautiful' (*thaumaston kalon*),[1] of 'divine Beauty' (*theion kalon*).[2] The onlooker becomes ecstatic, is seized by awe and terror (*ekplettontai*). A 'madness' takes hold of him.[3] Plato's metaphysics of beauty is in sharp contrast to the modern aesthetics of beauty; the latter is an aesthetics of pleasure which confirms the subject in its autonomy and complacency, instead of shocking it.

The aesthetics of beauty in modern times fittingly begins with the *aesthetics of the smooth*. For Edmund Burke, beautiful is first of all what is *smooth*. The bodies which provide pleasure for the sense of touch should not offer any *resistance*. They must be smooth. Thus, the smooth is an *optimized* surface *without negativity*. It causes a sensation which is entirely free of pain or resistance:

If it appears that smoothness is a principal cause of pleasure to the touch, taste, smell, and hearing, it will be easily admitted a constituent of visual beauty; especially as we have before shown, that this quality is found almost without exception in all bodies that are by gen-

16

eral consent held beautiful. There can be no doubt that bodies which are rough and angular, rouse and vellicate the organs of feeling, causing a sense of pain, which consists in the violent tension or contraction of the muscular fibres.[4]

The negativity of pain reduces the sense of beauty. Even 'robustness and strength'[5] lower its intensity. Beautiful traits include 'delicacy and speciousness'.[6] The body is 'elegant' if it consists of 'parts smooth and polished', parts not 'shewing any ruggedness or confusion'.[7] A beautiful body which evokes love and satisfaction does not give rise to the anticipation of resistance. The mouth is slightly opened, the breathing is slow, the whole body is at rest and the hands are carelessly hanging down on either side of the body. And all this, says Burke, is 'accompanied with an inward sense of melting and languor'.[8]

Burke makes the smooth an essential characteristic of the beautiful. Thus, smooth leaves on trees and flowers, and the smooth feathers or furs of animals, are beautiful. It is in particular her smooth skin that makes a woman beautiful. Any roughness diminishes beauty:

For, take any beautiful object, and give it a broken and rugged surface; and however well formed it may be in other respects, it pleases no longer. Whereas, let it want ever so many of the other constituents, if it wants not this, it becomes more pleasing than almost all the others without it.[9]

A sharp angle also diminishes beauty: 'For indeed any ruggedness, any sudden projection, any sharp angle, is in the highest degree contrary to that idea.'[10] Although a discontinuity in a form, like any variation, increases beauty, it must not be too abrupt or sudden. Beauty will only tolerate a gentle change in form: 'these [angular] figures, it is true, vary greatly; yet they vary in a sudden and broken manner; and I do not find any natural object which is angular, and at the same time beautiful'.[11]

With regard to the sense of taste, sweetness corresponds to smoothness: 'In the smell and taste, we find all things agreeable to them, and which are commonly called sweet, to be of a smooth nature, . . .'[12] The smooth and the sweet have the same origin. They are phenomena of pure positivity, and thus they exhaust themselves in mere pleasure.

Edmund Burke releases beauty of any negativity. It must provide an altogether 'positive pleasure'.[13] The sublime, by contrast, has an inherent negativity. The beautiful is small and delicate, luminous and tender. It is characterized by smoothness and flatness. The sublime is large, massive, grim, rough and coarse. It causes pain and terror. But it is healthy insofar as it violently moves the soul [*Gemüt*], while beauty causes it to relax. In the face of the sublime, Burke lets the negativity of pain and terror reverse back into positivity; it is a negativity with a purifying and enlivening effect. Thus, the sublime stands fully at the service of the subject. It thereby loses its *otherness* and *alien nature*. It is absorbed in its entirety by the subject:

> In all these cases, if the pain and terror are so modified as not to be actually noxious; if the pain is not carried to violence, and the terror is not conversant about the

present destruction of the person, as these emotions clear the parts, whether fine or gross, of a dangerous and troublesome encumbrance, they are capable of producing delight; not pleasure, but a sort of delightful horror, a sort of tranquillity tinged with terror; . . .[14]

Like Burke, Kant isolates beauty in its positivity. It causes a positive pleasure. However, this pleasure exceeds the culinary kind as Kant makes it an integral part of the epistemological process. Imagination and understanding both participate in the production of knowledge. Imagination is the faculty which synthesizes the manifold sensual data presented by the intuition into a coherent *picture*. The understanding operates at one level of abstraction above that. It subsumes the pictures under *concepts*. In the case of beauty, the cognitive faculties of the imagination and understanding are in a state of free *play*, in harmonious interplay. When looking at something beautiful, the cognitive faculties *play*. They do not yet *work* on the production of knowledge. In other words, when faced with beauty, the cognitive faculties are in play mode. However, their free play [*Spiel*] is not entirely free, not free of purpose, because it is a *prelude* [*Vorspiel*] to knowledge as *work*. But here they still *play*. Beauty presupposes *play*. It is situated at a preliminary stage to *work*.

The subject likes beauty because beauty stimulates the harmonious interplay of the cognitive faculties. The sensation of beauty is nothing but the 'pleasure in the harmony of the faculties of cognition',[15] in the harmonious 'disposition of the cognitive powers',[16] which is essential for the *work* of cognition. Ultimately, Kant subordinates play to work, even to 'business'.[17] Beauty may

19

not produce knowledge by itself, but it *keeps* the machinery of cognition *moving*. Faced with beauty, the subject likes *itself*. The beautiful is an autoerotic feeling. It is not an object-feeling, but a subject-feeling. Beauty is not the *other* by which the subject would allow itself to be swept away. The pleasure in beauty is the pleasure of the subject in itself. Adorno, in his *Aesthetic Theory*, emphasizes precisely the autoerotic element in Kant's aesthetic of beauty: 'This formal principle, obedient to subjective lawfulness regardless of what is other to it, and unshaken by its other, continues to give pleasure: In it subjectivity, unconscious of itself, enjoys the feeling of power.'[18]

As opposed to beauty, the sublime does not cause an immediate feeling of pleasure. As in Burke, the initial sensation in reaction to the sublime is pain or displeasure. The sublime is too enormous, too huge for the imagination, which cannot capture it and is unable to condense it into a picture. Thus, the subject is shocked and overwhelmed by it. This is what constitutes the negativity of the sublime. When looking at vast natural phenomena, the subject initially feels powerless. But it regains its composure through that 'self-preservation of quite another kind'.[19] It takes refuge in the inwardness of reason and its idea of infinity compared to which 'everything in nature is small'.[20]

Even powerful natural phenomena do not shock the subject. Reason remains aloof to them. The fear of death, the 'inhibition of the vital powers' when faced with the sublime,[21] is only of short duration. The retreat into the inwardness of reason and its ideas turns it into the feeling of pleasure again:

Thus the wide ocean, enraged by storms, cannot be called sublime. Its visage is horrible; and one must already have filled the mind with all sorts of ideas if by means of such an intuition it is to be put in the mood for a feeling which is itself sublime, in that the mind is incited to abandon sensibility and to occupy itself with ideas that contain a higher purposiveness.[22]

Faced with the sublime [*Erhabene*], the subject feels superior [*erhaben*] to nature, because what is truly sublime is the idea of infinity which is inherent to reason. This sublimity is erroneously projected on to an object, in this case on to nature. Kant calls this confusion a 'subreption'.[23] The sublime, like beauty, is not an object-, but a subject-feeling, an autoerotic feeling of the self.

The pleasure in the sublime is 'negative',[24] whereas 'that in the beautiful is positive'.[25] The pleasure in the beautiful is positive because the subject immediately likes it. When faced with the sublime, the subject initially experiences displeasure. This is why the pleasure in the sublime is negative. The negativity of the sublime does not consist in the fact that it confronts the subject with the *other of itself*, that it *pulls the subject out of itself* and towards the other, that the subject ends up *beside itself*. No negativity of the *other* which would cross out the autoeroticism of the subject is inherent in the sublime. Neither when faced with beauty, nor when faced with the sublime, does the subject end up *beside itself*. It permanently remains grounded *in itself*. Anything that would be wholly other, and would evade the sublime, Kant would consider dreadful, monstrous or abysmal. It would be a disaster for which there is no place in Kant's aesthetics.

21

Neither beauty nor the sublime represents the *other* of the subject. Rather, they are absorbed by the inwardness of the subject. We may recuperate *another* beauty, even a *beauty of the other*, only if we grant it a place *beyond autoerotic subjectivity*. The attempt, however, to put beauty under the general suspicion of being the seed of consumer culture, and to play it off against the sublime in postmodern fashion, is not helpful.[26] Beauty and the sublime have the same origin. Instead of opposing the sublime to the beautiful, one should return to beauty a sublimity that cannot be subjected to inwardness, a *de-subjectivizing* sublimity, and thus undo the separation of beauty and the sublime.

4

Digital Beauty

Kant's subject remains within itself at all times. It never loses itself, or exhausts itself. An autoerotic inwardness protects it against any intrusion from the other or the outside. Nothing can shock it. Adorno is thinking of another kind of mind, one that, when faced with the sublime in nature, becomes aware of what is *wholly other* about itself. The sublime tears the subject out of its captivity in itself:

> Rather than that, as Kant thought, spirit in the face of nature becomes aware of its own superiority, it becomes aware of its own natural essence. This is the moment when the subject, vis-à-vis the sublime, is moved to tears. Recollection of nature breaks the arrogance of his self-positing: 'My tears well up; earth, I am returning to you.' With that, the self exits, spiritually, from its imprisonment in itself.[1]

The tears break '[t]he spell that the subject casts over nature'.[2] Crying, it steps outside of itself. For Adorno, a genuine aesthetic experience is not one of pleasure in which the subject recognizes itself, but one in which it is shocked, or realizes its own finitude:

> Shudder, radically opposed to the conventional idea of experience [*Erlebnis*], provides no particular satisfaction for the I; it bears no similarity to desire. Rather, it is a memento of the liquidation of the I, which, shaken, perceives its own limitedness and finitude.[3]

'Natural beauty' is not something that is immediately liked. It does not refer to a beautiful landscape:

> The 'How beautiful!' at the sight of a landscape insults its mute language and reduces its beauty; appearing nature wants silence ... The more intensively one observes nature, the less one is aware of its beauty, unless it was already involuntarily recognized.[4]

Natural beauty is revealed to *blind, unconscious* perception. As 'the cipher of the not-yet-existing',[5] it refers to 'what appears to be more than what is literally there'.[6] Adorno speaks of '[t]he shame felt in the face of natural beauty' which stems from 'the damage implicitly done to what does not yet exist by taking it for existent. The dignity of nature is that of the not-yet-existing; by its expression it repels intentional humanization.' It rejects any kind of being used. Thus, natural beauty altogether evades consumption, as well as 'communication', which only leads to 'the adaptation of spirit to utility, with the

24

result that spirit is made one commodity among the rest; . . .'[7]

To pure pleasure, which is always tinged with auto-eroticism, natural beauty remains closed off. Only *pain* has access to it. Pain *tears* the subject *out* of its auto-erotic inwardness. Pain is the *tear* which announces what is wholly other: 'The pain in the face of beauty, nowhere more visceral than in the experience of nature, is as much the longing for what beauty promises . . .'[8] The longing for natural beauty is ultimately the longing for a different mode of being, for another, altogether non-violent form of life.

Natural beauty is opposed to digital beauty. In digital beauty the negativity of the *other* is entirely removed. It is therefore perfectly *smooth*. It is not meant to contain any *tear*. Its signature is pleasure without any negativity, namely the *Like*. Digital beauty forms a *smooth space of the same*, which does not permit anything alien, any *alterity*, to enter. The pure *inside* without any exteriority is the mode in which it appears. It turns even nature into a *window* of itself. Thanks to the total digitalization of being, there is a total subjectivizing, an *absolute subjectivity* under which the human being only encounters itself.

The temporality of natural beauty is the *already of the not-yet*. It appears on the utopian horizon of what is *coming*. The temporality of digital beauty, by contrast, is the immediate present without a *future*, even without *history*. It *simply is present*, while a distance is inherent to natural beauty: the latter 'veils itself at the moment of greatest proximity'.[9] Its auratic distance removes it from any kind of consumption:

25

> As indeterminate, as antithetical to definitions, natural
> beauty is indefinable, and in this it is related to music,
> . . . Just as in music what is beautiful flashes up in nature
> only to disappear in the instant one tries to grasp it.[10]

Natural beauty and artistic beauty are not opposed to each other. Rather, art imitates 'natural beauty as such'[11] – 'what is unutterable in the language of nature'.[12] In doing so, it saves it. Artistic beauty is the 'afterimage of the silence that is the single medium through which nature speaks'.[13]

Natural beauty turns out to be 'the trace of the non-identical in things under the spell of universal identity'.[14] Digital beauty banishes any negativity of the non-identical. It only permits consumable, usable *differences*. *Alterity* gives way to *diversity*. The digital world, in a manner of speaking, is a world that the humans have coated over with their own retina. This humanly *networked* world produces a permanent self-mirroring. The closer the net is woven, the more thoroughly the world shields itself against the other, the outside. The digital retina turns the world into a screen-and-control monitor. Inside this autoerotic visual space, in this *digital inwardness* there can be no sense of wonder. The only thing human beings still like are themselves.

5

The Aesthetics of Veiling

Beauty is a hideout. Concealment is essential to beauty. Transparency and beauty do not go together. *Transparent beauty* is oxymoronic. Beauty is necessarily *semblance.* *Opacity* is inherent to it. *Opaque* means shaded. Unveiling disenchants and destroys beauty. Thus, it lies in the nature of beauty that it *cannot be unveiled.*

Pornography – as nakedness without any drapes, without any secrets – is the opposite figure to beauty. Its ideal place is the shop window:

Nothing more homogeneous than a pornographic photograph. It is always a naïve photograph, without intention and without calculation. Like a shop window which shows only one illuminated piece of jewelry, it is completely constituted by the presentation of only one

27

thing: sex: no secondary, untimely object ever manages
to half conceal, delay, or distract ...[1]

Concealing, delaying and distracting are also spatio-
temporal strategies of beauty. The calculation in half-
concealing produces a seductive gloss. The beautiful
hesitates before appearing. Distraction protects it against
direct contact. It is essential to eroticism. Pornography is
without any distraction. It gets right down to it. Distraction
transforms pornography into erotic photography:

> A proof *a contrario:* Mapplethorpe shifts his close-ups of
> genitalia from the pornographic to the erotic by photo-
> graphing the fabric of underwear at very close range: the
> photograph is no longer unary, since I am interested in
> the texture of the material.[2]

The photographer takes care to distract from the *object*. He
turns the secondary object into the main object, or subordinates the latter to the former. Beauty also takes place
beside the object [*Sache*], in the marginal [*Nebensächliche*].
The *beautiful object* does not exist.

According to Walter Benjamin, Goethe's poetry is
'turned toward the interior in the veiled light refracted
through multicolored panes'. The veil affected Goethe
again and again 'where he was struggling for insight into
beauty'.[3] Benjamin quotes from Goethe's *Faust*:

> Hold tight to what of all of it is left you
> The dress, don't let it go. Demons already
> Are tugging at the ends, would dearly like
> To haul it away to the underworld. Hold tight.

28

It is no longer the goddess – you have lost her –
But is divine.[4]

It is the dress that is divine. The veiling is essential for
beauty. Thus, beauty cannot be undressed or unveiled.
The impossibility of unveiling beauty is its nature.

What is beautiful is the object in its draping, in its
veil, its hideout. The beautiful object remains true to
itself only under its veil. Unveiled, it becomes 'infinitely
inconspicuous [*unscheinbar*]'.[5] To be beautiful categori-
cally means to be veiled. Benjamin therefore demands of
art criticism a *hermeneutics of veiling*:

> The task of art criticism is not to lift the veil but rather,
> through the most precise knowledge of it as a veil, to
> raise itself for the first time to the true view of the beau-
> tiful. To the view that will never open itself to so-called
> empathy, and will only imperfectly open itself to a purer
> contemplation of the naïve: to the view of the beautiful
> as that which is secret. Never yet has a true work of
> art been grasped other than where it ineluctably repre-
> sented itself as a secret. For that object, to which in the
> last instance the veil is essential, is not to be character-
> ized otherwise.[6]

Beauty neither conveys itself to direct empathy nor to
naïve contemplation. Both are approaches that try to lift
the veil, or to look through the veil. The only way to view
beauty as a secret is through *knowledge of the veil as such*.
One needs first of all to turn towards the veil in order to
recognize what is veiled. The veil is more essential than
the veiled object.

The veiling also eroticizes the text. God, Augustine says, intentionally obscures the Holy Scripture through the use of metaphorical style, burying things 'under figures of speech',[7] in order to make them an object of desire. The *beautiful dress* of metaphors eroticizes the scriptures. Thus, the dress is essential to the scriptures, even to the beautiful. The technique of veiling turns hermeneutics into eroticism. It maximizes the *pleasure of the text* and turns reading into an act of love.

The Torah also uses the technique of veiling. The text is represented as a lover who hides herself and only for an instant [*Augenblick*] unveils her face to the one she loves, who himself remains hidden. Reading turns into an erotic adventure:

> Verily the Torah lets out a word and emerges a little from her sheath, and then hides herself again. But she does this only for those who know and obey her. For the Torah resembles a beautiful and stately damsel, who is hidden in a secluded chamber of her palace and who has a secret lover, unknown to all others. For love of her he keeps passing the gate of her house, looking this way and that in search of her. She knows that her lover haunts the gate of her house. What does she do? She opens the door of her hidden chamber ever so little, and for a moment reveals her face to her lover, but hides it again forthwith.[8]

The Torah 'reveals herself and hides': 'through a light veil she speaks allegorical words'.[9] To her love she tells 'of all her hidden secrets and all her hidden ways, which have been in her heart from the beginning'.[10]

30

Information, by definition, cannot be veiled. It is transparent by nature. Information simply is given. It repels any metaphor, any veiling dress. It speaks *straight out*. This is also what distinguishes it from *knowledge* which can retreat into secrecy. Information follows an altogether different principle. It is directed towards revealing, towards the ultimate truth. Information has a pornographic nature.

For Barthes, veiling is an essential part of eroticism. The 'most erotic portion' of a body is 'where the garment gapes',[11] that piece of skin which flashes 'between two articles of clothing (trousers and sweater), between two edges (the open-necked shirt, the glove and the sleeve)'. What is erotic is the 'staging of an appearance-as-disappearing'.[12] Tear, break and gap account for the erotic. The erotic pleasure of a text differs from the 'pleasure of the corporeal striptease' which derives from a *progressive unveiling*.[13] A catchy novel which moves towards a final unveiling, a *final truth*, is also pornographic: 'the entire excitation takes refuge in the *hope* of seeing the sexual organ (schoolboy's dream) or in knowing the end of the story (novelistic satisfaction)'.[14] The erotic can do *without truth*. It is semblance, a phenomenon pertaining to the veil.

Seduction is 'founded upon my intuition of something in the other that remains forever secret for him, something that I can never know directly about him but which nevertheless exercises a fascination upon me from behind its veil of secrecy'.[15] A 'pathos of distance',[16] even a *pathos of veiling*, is inherent to seduction. The intimacy provided by love already diminishes the secret distance which is crucial in seduction. The pornographic film, finally, lets it disappear altogether:

From one figure to the other, from seduction to love, then to desire, sexuality, finally to pure and simple porno; the farther you go, the closer you come to the lesser secret, the smaller enigma, towards avowal, expression, unveiling, . . .[17]

Not only is the body laid bare, but also the soul. Pornography of the soul marks the absolute end to seduction which is more play than *truth*.

6

The Aesthetics of Injury

Roland Barthes has in mind an *eroticism of harm*: 'I have no skin (except for caresses). Parodying Socrates in the *Phaedrus*, one should speak of the Flayed Man, and not the Feathered Man, in matters of love.'[1] The eroticism of having no skin is based on a radical passivity. The exposure of the flayed exceeds even that of the denuded. It means *pain* and *harm*: 'flayed. The particular sensibility of the amorous subject, which renders him vulnerable, defenseless to the slightest injuries.'[2]

Today's society of positivity forever reduces the negativity of harm. This also applies to love. Any major commitment that might lead to injury is avoided. Libidinal energies are distributed across many objects, like capital investments, in order to avoid a total loss. Perception also increasingly avoids negativity. It is dominated by the *Like*. But *seeing* in the emphatic sense always means *seeing differently*, namely *experiencing*. It is impossible to see differently without exposing oneself to injury. Seeing requires vulnerability. Otherwise the same keeps on repeating itself. Sensibility is vulnerability. One might also say that injury is the *moment of truth in seeing*. Without injury there is no truth [*Wahrheit*], not even perception [Wahr*nehmen*]. There is no truth in the *hell of the same*.

In *The Notebooks of Malte Laurids Brigge*, Rilke describes *seeing* as an injury. Seeing exposes itself totally to what enters into the unknown zones of my ego. Thus, learning how to see is anything but an active, conscious process. Rather, it is a *letting-happen* or an *exposing-oneself-to-what-happens*:

> I'm learning how to see. I don't know what the reason is, but everything enters into me more deeply and no longer stops at the point where it used to come to an end. I have an inner self that I knew nothing about. Now everything goes into it. I don't know what happens there.[3]

The negativity of being shocked and moved – that is, the negativity of injury – is a necessary part of *experience*. Experience resembles a crossing during which one must expose oneself to a danger:

> the hérisson [*hedgehog*]. It blinds itself ... sensing the danger on the autoroute, it exposes itself to an accident ... No poem without accident, no poem that does not open itself like a wound, but no poem that is not also just as wounding.[4]

34

Without injury, neither poetry nor art is possible. Thinking is also sparked by the negativity of injury. Without pain and injury, the same, the familiar, the habitual continue: 'experience is in essence the suffering in which the essential otherness of beings reveals itself in opposition to the tried and usual'.[5]

Barthes's theory of photography also develops an aesthetic of injury. Barthes distinguishes between two elements of photography. The first one he calls '*studium*', and it is concerned with the vast field of information which needs to be studied, the 'field of unconcerned desire, of various interest, of inconsequential taste: *I like / I don't like*'.[6] The observer browses and takes pleasurable walks through the field of the *studium*. He or she indulges in photography as a feast for the eyes. The *studium* belongs to the category of the '*to like*', the *I-like-it*, and not the category of the '*to love*'. The '*to like*' lacks any intensity, any quality of a shock.

Photography is culturally coded.[7] The *studium* follows this code more or less joyfully, but this is 'never my delight or my pain'.[8] It does not spark any passion or love; it only 'mobilizes a half desire, a demi-volition', and is guided by a 'vague, slippery, irresponsible interest'.[9]

The second element of photography is the '*punctum*'. The *punctum* injures, wounds, shocks the observer: 'This time it is not I who seek it out (as I invest the field of the *studium* with my sovereign consciousness), it is this element which rises from the scene, shoots out of it like an arrow, and pierces me.'[10] The *punctum*, suddenly, holds all of my attention. The reading of the *punctum* is 'brief and active, crouched like a beast of prey before it pounces'.[11] The *punctum* announces itself as a gaze, the gaze of a

35

beast of prey which looks at me, which calls the authority of my eyes into question. It riddles the photograph as a *feast for the eyes*.

The *punctum* marks a *gap in vision*, a 'blind field'.[12] Thus, the photography which contains a *punctum* is a *hideout*. This is what constitutes its eroticism, its seductive power:

> The presence (the dynamics) of this blind field is, I believe, what distinguishes the erotic photograph from the pornographic photograph. . . . for me, there is no *punctum* in the pornographic image; at most it amuses me (and even then, boredom follows quickly).[13]

The erotic photograph is a picture 'that has been disturbed, fissured'.[14] The pornographic photograph, by contrast, has neither fractures nor fissures. It is *smooth*. Today all pictures are more or less pornographic. They are transparent. They do not present gaps in the field of vision. They contain no hideouts.

A fundamental lack of transparency is a further aspect of the *punctum*. It evades any naming or signification. It cannot be transformed into either information or knowledge: 'What I can name cannot really prick me. The incapacity to name is a good symptom of disturbance.'[15] The *punctum* finds me where I am unknown to myself. This is what makes for its *uncanniness*: 'The effect is certain but unlocatable, it does not find its sign, its name; it is sharp and yet lands in a vague zone of myself; . . .'[16]

Unary photographs lack a *punctum*. They are merely objects for *studium*. Despite the negativity of injuring, the *punctum* differs from a shock:

36

News photographs are very often unary (the unary photograph is not necessarily tranquil). In these images, no *punctum:* a certain shock – the literal can traumatize – but no disturbance; the photograph can 'shout,' not wound.[17]

As opposed to a shock, a *punctum* does not *shout*. It loves to remain silent, to keep the secret. Despite its stillness it finds expression as an injury. Once all meanings, intentions, opinions, evaluations, judgments, enactments, poses, gestures, codifications and information are done with, the *punctum* reveals itself as a *quiet, singing remainder* which *affects* us. The *punctum* is the resisting residue which is left behind by *representation*, an immediacy that evades being mediated by sense and signification, the corporeal, the material, the affective, the unconscious, even the *real* as opposed to the *symbolic*.

Due to their mode of temporality, cinematographic images do not possess a *punctum*:

> in front of the screen, I am not free to shut my eyes; otherwise, opening them again, I would not discover the same image; I am constrained to a continuous voracity; a host of other qualities, but not *pensiveness*; whence the interest, for me, of the photogram.[18]

The greedy consumption of images makes it impossible to close the eyes. The *punctum* presupposes an *ascetic vision*. Something musical is inherent in it. This music only rings out once the eyes are closed 'in a state, an effort, of silence'.[19] The stillness frees the image of the 'usual blah-blah' of communication.[20] The closing of the

37

eyes means 'to make the image speak in silence'.[21] Thus, Barthes quotes Kafka saying: "'We photograph things in order to drive them out of our minds. My stories are a way of shutting my eyes.'"[22] The *punctum* evades being immediately perceived. It slowly matures in the space of the imagination which unfolds while closing the eyes. In this space, secret correspondences between things take place. The language of the *punctum* is a *dream protocol of the imagination*.

In the course of acceleration, immediate presence becomes total. It pushes out any latency. Everything has to be available at once. The *punctum* does not reveal itself at once, but only in the hindsight of remembering:

> Nothing surprising, then, if sometimes, despite its clarity, the *punctum* should be revealed only after the fact, when the photograph is no longer in front of me and I think back on it. I may know better a photograph I remember than a photograph I am looking at, . . . I had just realized that however immediate and incisive it was, the *punctum* could accommodate a certain latency (but never any scrutiny).[23]

The perception of digital images takes place in the form of contagion, being affected, as immediate contact between image and eye. This constitutes its obscenity. It lacks any *aesthetic* distance. Perception as contagion does not permit the closing of one's eyes. Barthes's conceptual pair *studium/punctum* is to be complemented with the *affectum*. The immediate contact between image and eye no longer allows for anything other than the *affectum*. The digital medium is a *medium of the affect*. Affects are quicker than feelings or discourses. They accelerate communication. The *affectum* does not know of any patience for *studium*, or of any receptivity for the *punctum*. It lacks the eloquent stillness, the *communicative* silence, which accounts for the *punctum*. The affectum *shouts* and *excites*. All it produces are non-verbal excitement and stimuli, which cause an immediate liking.

7

The Aesthetics of Disaster

In Kant's *Critique of Practical Reason*, we find the famous adage which is also written on his gravestone: 'Two things fill the mind with ever new and increasing admiration and reverence, the more often and more steadily one reflects on them: *the starry heavens above me and the moral law within me*.'[1] The moral law is at home in reason. And the starry night also does not represent an outside; it is not outside the subject. It stretches across the *inwardness of reason*. *Disaster* means literally *ill-starred* (from Latin *des-astrum*).

The disaster is unknown to Kant. Even vast natural phenomena do not represent disastrous events. Faced with the power of nature, the subject seeks refuge in the *inwardness* of reason which makes everything *outside* appear small. Kant permanently immunizes himself against an *outside* which evades the autoerotic inwardness

40

of the subject. Everything is meant to be put under the spell of the subject's inner world – this is the categorical imperative of Kant's thought.

According to Hegel, the task of art is 'to convert every shape in all points of its visible surface into an eye',[2] in which 'the free soul is revealed in its inner infinity'.[3]

> Or, as Plato cries out to the star in his familiar distich: 'When thou lookest on the stars, my star, oh! would I were the heavens and could see thee with a thousand eyes', so, conversely, art makes every one of its productions into a thousand-eyed Argus, whereby the inner soul and spirit is seen at every point.[4]

Spirit is itself a thousand-eyed Argus which illuminates all without exception. Hegel's heaven of a thousand eyes resembles Kant's starry heavens which are not beset by any *unlucky star* or *outside*. Hegel's 'spirit' as well as Kant's 'reason' represent incantations against *disaster*, against the *outside*, against the *wholly other*.

The disaster intrudes upon the 'starry space' as an unlucky star. It is the 'radical heterogeneity',[5] the outside, which breaks open the inwardness of spirit: 'I will not say that the disaster is absolute; on the contrary, it disorients the absolute. It comes and goes, errant disarray, and yet with the imperceptible but intense suddenness of the outside, . . .'[6] The disaster is characterized by an alertness which differs from Hegel's 'thousand-eyed Argus': 'If I say: the disaster keeps watch, it is not in order to give a subject to the vigil; it is to say: the wake does not occur under the sidereal sky.'[7] The disaster means a 'withdrawal outside the sidereal abode'.[8]

For Blanchot, the empty sky as the counter-image to the starry heavens represents the primal scene of his childhood. This sky reveals to him the a-topicality of what is wholly other, an outside that cannot be internalized, and whose beauty and sublimity fill the child with a 'devastating joy':

> the sky, the same sky, suddenly open, absolutely black and absolutely empty . . . The unexpected aspect of this scene (its interminable feature) is the feeling of happiness (bonheur) that straightaway submerges the child, the ravaging joy to which he can bear witness only in tears, an endless flood of tears.[9]

The child is in raptures over the infinity of the empty sky. Torn out of its inwardness, it is shifted to an a-topical outside and thus moved beyond boundaries and emptied. The disaster proves to be a formula for happiness.

The aesthetics of disaster contradicts an aesthetics of pleasure where the object of the subject's enjoyment is the subject itself. The aesthetics of disaster is an *aesthetics of the event*. Inconspicuous events such as white dust swirled up by a drop of rain, snow falling silently in the morning twilight, or a scent coming off a rock in the summer heat, all these can also be disastrous events, namely *events of emptiness* which empty the ego, de-subjectify it and take away its inwardness, thus making it happy. These events are *beautiful* because they *expropriate* the ego. A disaster means the death of the autoerotic subject which clings to itself.

Baudelaire's *Les Fleurs du mal* contains the poem *Hymne à la Beauté*. The stars (*des astres*) out of which beauty rises,

Baudelaire rhymes with disaster (*désastres*). Beauty is a disaster which upsets the order of the stars. It is the torch (*flambeau*) which the butterfly approaches and in which it burns to death. *Flambeau* rhymes with *tombeau* (grave). Beauty (*beau*) is inscribed into the *flambeau* as well as the *tombeau*. The negativity of disaster, of what is deadly, is a moment of beauty.

Beauty, Rainer Maria Rilke's first *Duino Elegy* says, 'is nothing but the beginning of terror, which we still are just able to endure'.[10] The negativity of terror forms the matrix, the deep layer of beauty. What is beautiful is the still just bearable unbearable, or the unbearable that has been made bearable. It shields us from the terrible. But, at the same time, the terrible can be seen through the beautiful. This is what constitutes the ambivalence of beauty. Beauty is not an image, but a *shield*.

For Adorno, too, the negativity of terror is essential to beauty. Beauty is the form which inscribes itself into the formless, into what is undifferentiated: 'Of that on which it was active the aesthetically forming spirit allowed entry only to what resembled it, what it understood, or what it hoped to make like itself. This was a process of formalization; . . .'[11] The beautiful sets itself off from the formless, from the terrible, from undifferentiated totalities, by positing forms, i.e. differences: 'The image of beauty as that of a single and differentiated something originates with the emancipation from the fear of the overpowering wholeness and undifferentiatedness of nature.'[12] However, the semblance of beauty does not banish the terrible altogether. It does not fully succeed in 'making itself impervious to the immediately existent', to the formless.[13] Beauty 'digs in on the perimeter like the enemy in front of the walls of the beleaguered city and starves it out'.[14]

The semblance of beauty is fragile and threatened; it is 'progressively destroyed'[15] by its *other*, the terrible: 'The reduction that beauty imposes on the terrifying, over and out of which beauty raises itself and which it banishes from itself as from a sacred temple, has – in the face of the terrifying – something powerless about it.'[16] The relationship between the beautiful and the terrible is ambivalent. The beautiful does not simply reject the terrible. It does not discredit it. Rather the spirit which forms needs the formless, its enemy, in order not to ossify into dead semblance. Forming *rationality* is dependent on *mimesis* which adjusts itself to the formless and the terrible. Inherent to spirit is the 'longing for the vanquished',[17] which is nothing but the terrible. Beauty is located between disaster and depression, between the terrible and undead, between the intrusion of the other and freezing into the same. Adorno's idea of natural beauty is precisely a turn against the rigid identity of form. It bears witness to the non-identical:

Natural beauty is the trace of the nonidentical in things under the spell of universal identity. As long as this spell prevails, the nonidentical has no positive existence. Therefore natural beauty remains as dispersed and uncertain as what it promises, that which surpasses all human immanence.[18]

The negativity of being refracted [*Gebrochenheit*] is constitutive for beauty. Thus, Adorno speaks of artefacts' 'coherence, however self-antagonistic and refracted'.[19] Without the negativity of being refracted, beauty atrophies into the smooth. Adorno describes aesthetic form in paradoxical formulas. Its coherence, he says, consists in the fact 'that it does not cohere'; it is not free of 'divergences and contradictions'.[20] Its unity is broken. It is interrupted 'through its other'.[21] The heart of beauty, it is a broken heart.

The *healthy* is a form of expression of the smooth. Paradoxically, it radiates something morbid, something lifeless. Without the negativity of death, life solidifies into something dead. It is smoothened out into the undead. Negativity is the invigorating force of life. It also forms the essence of beauty. Inherent to beauty is a *weakness*, a *fragility*, and a *brokenness* [*Gebrochenheit*]. To this negativity, beauty owes its power to seduce. The healthy, by contrast, does not seduce. It has something pornographic about it. *Beauty is illness*:

> Exuberant health is always, as such, sickness also. Its antidote is a sickness aware of what it is, a curbing of life itself. Beauty is such a curative sickness. It arrests life, and therefore its decay. If, however, sickness is rejected for the sake of life, then hypostasized life, in its blind separation from its other moment, becomes the latter, destructiveness and evil, insolence and braggadocio. To hate destructiveness, one must hate life as well: only death is an image of undistorted life.[22]

Today's kalocracy which considers the healthy, the smooth as absolute values, eliminates beauty. And the mere, healthy life, which today takes the form of a hysterical survival, turns into something dead, into the undead. *Thus, we are today too dead to live, and too alive to die.*

45

8

The Ideal of Beauty

Although Kant's aesthetic of beauty is determined by autoerotic subjectivity, it is not yet an aesthetic of consumption. Kant's subject is of an ascetic rather than culinary disposition. The pleasure felt in perceiving beauty is *disinterested*. There is an *aesthetic* distance which enables a contemplative lingering with beauty. Aesthetic intuition is not consumptive but contemplative. Although Kant isolates beauty in its positivity, it is not yet an object for culinary pleasure. Beauty does not emit an attractive *stimulus*. Rather, it is an aesthetic *form*. Today's aesthetic regime, by contrast, produces a vast amount of stimuli. It is precisely this flood of stimuli and excitement that makes beauty disappear. It does not permit any contemplative distance towards the object and surrenders it to consumption.

Furthermore, in Kant, beauty exceeds the purely aesthetic. It reaches into the moral realm. In his poem, *Hymne an die Schönheit* [Hymn to beauty], Hölderlin invokes Kant: 'In its beautiful forms Nature speaks to us figuratively, and the gift of deciphering its secret writing has been given to us in our moral feeling.'[1] The moral surplus value of beauty also accounts for the 'ideal of beauty'[2] which Kant distinguishes from the 'normal idea of beauty'. The normal idea of beauty is a species-specific norm.[3] A shape appears beautiful if it conforms to this norm, and ugly if it altogether deviates from it. Not only the human species but any species has its own normal idea of beauty. It is 'merely the correctness in the presentation of the species', an 'archetype' according to which a species reproduces itself.[4] A face which corresponds to the normal idea of beauty is a perfectly regular, smooth face which 'cannot contain anything specifically characteristic'.[5] It 'expresses more the idea of the species than anything specific to a person'.[6] As opposed to the normal idea of beauty, the 'ideal of beauty' is unique to the human species. It is the 'visible expression of moral ideas, which inwardly govern human beings'.[7]

Due to the substance of reason it contains, the ideal of beauty evades any form of being consumed: 'no sensory charm is allowed to be mixed into the satisfaction in its object, while it nevertheless allows a great interest to be taken in it'.[8] The judgement pertaining to the ideal of beauty exceeds the purely aesthetic and mere taste. It is an 'intellectualized judgement of taste' which rests on the 'unification of taste with reason, i.e., of the beautiful with the good'.[9] Not everyone is capable of representing and judging such beauty. To do so requires a power of the imagination capable of visualizing the moral ideas which were imparted in the course of an advanced education. In the form of his ideal of beauty, Kant conceives of a *moral beauty* or a *morality of the beautiful.*

Historically, for a long time, beauty was only relevant to the extent that it expressed morality and character. Today, the beautiful character gives way entirely to sexiness:

> Nineteenth-century middle-class women were viewed as attractive because of their beauty, less because of what we would call today their sexual appeal. Beauty was viewed as a physical and spiritual attribute. . . . Sexual appeal as such did not represent a legitimate criterion for mate selection and in that respect represents a new criterion of evaluation, detached both from beauty and from moral character, or rather in which character and psychological makeup are ultimately subsumed under sexiness.[10]

The sexualization of the body does not follow the logic of emancipation in a one-sided fashion, because it takes place alongside the commercialization of the body. The beauty industry exploits the body by sexualizing it and making it fit as an object to be consumed. Consumption and sexiness condition each other. The self that is based on sexual desire is a product of consumer capitalism. Consumer culture more and more submits beauty to the schemata of stimuli and excitement. The ideal of beauty evades consumption. Thus, any surplus-value beauty is removed. Beauty becomes smooth and submits to consumption.

Sexiness is opposed to moral beauty or beauty of character. Morality, virtue and character have a specific temporality. They are based on duration, solidity and permanence. The original meaning of character is the sign that is burnt-in, the irremovable branded sign. Its main trait is its immutability. For Carl Schmitt, water is an element that lacks character to the extent that it does not allow for fixed markings: 'On the sea . . . firm lines cannot be engraved. . . . The sea has no character, in the original sense of the word, which comes from the Greek *charassein*, meaning to engrave, to scratch, to imprint.'[11]

Solidity and permanence are not conducive to consumption. Consumption and duration exclude each other. The impermanence and fleetingness of fashion, by contrast, accelerate consumption. Thus, the culture of consumption removes duration. Character and consumption are opposites. The *ideal consumer* is a person *without character*. Lack of character enables indiscriminate consumption.

According to Schmitt, it is 'a sign of inner conflict to have more than one real enemy'. A stable character does not allow for a 'doubling of the enemy'. It is necessary to engage with the one real enemy and 'fight him', 'in order to gain one's own measure, one's own limit, one's own shape'. Thus, the enemy is 'our own shape in the form of a question'.[12] Just one real friend would also be proof that one has a stable character. Schmitt would say, the less character and shape someone has, the smoother and slicker someone is, the more *Friends*[13] he or she has. *Facebook is a characterless market.*

Carl Schmitt's treatise on *The Nomos of the Earth* begins by giving praise to the earth. Schmitt praises it first of all for its solidity. The earth allows for clear boundaries, distinctions, enclosures. Its solidity also makes it possible to erect border stones, walls and fortresses:

> Then, the orders and orientations of human social life become apparent. Families, clans, tribes, estates, forms of ownership and neighbourly relations, also forms of power and domination, become publicly visible.[14]

Schmitt's 'nomos of the earth' is a paradigm which we have long since left behind in favour of the digital. The digital order shifts all parameters of *Being*. 'Forms of ownership', 'neighbourly relations', 'clans', 'tribes' and 'estates' all belong to the telluric order, the order of the earth. Digital networks dissolve clans, tribes and neighbourly relations. The sharing economy also makes 'ownership' superfluous by substituting it with *access*. The digital medium resembles the characterless sea on which no fixed lines and markings can be engraved. No fortresses, no thresholds, no walls, no moats, no boundary stones can be erected on the digital sea. Stable characters are difficult to network. They lack *connectivity and communication*. In times of networking, globalization and communication, a stable character can only be an obstacle and disadvantage. The digital order celebrates another ideal. It is called the *man without character, characterless smoothness*.

9

Beauty as Truth

Hegel's aesthetics, like Kant's, can be subjected to a double reading. On the one hand, it can be read from the perspective of subjective inwardness that does not know of any outside, or of any disaster. On the other hand, it allows for a reading which moves along the lines of freedom and reconciliation. This second reading is the more interesting of the two. If one takes Hegel's thought out of the corset of subjectivity, or breaks off the tip of subjectivity, it reveals some interesting aspects. The postmodern critique of Hegel completely ignores the theme of subjectivity.

Central to Hegel's aesthetics is the 'concept'. It idealizes beauty and confers on it the *brilliance of truth*. Beauty results from the concept manifesting itself in the sensual, or 'the Idea as the immediate unity of the Concept with its reality'.[1] Hegel's 'concept' is nothing abstract.

It is the living and enlivening form, which shapes reality by *reaching* all the way through it [*hin-durch*-greifend]. The concept unites the elements of reality into living, organic wholes. The totality formed by the concept *grasps* [*be*-greift] everything within it. Everything is *encapsulated* [*in-begriffen*] in the concept. This collection, this gathering into the *one*, which is capable of 'summoning back the innumerable individualities out of their dispersal in order to concentrate them into one expression and one shape', is *beautiful*.[2] The concept is gathering, mediating and reconciling. Thus, 'the concept is not applicable to an aggregate [*Haufen*; heap]'.[3] No 'aggregate' is beautiful. Concepts take care that wholes do not disintegrate, or dissipate, into 'heaps'.

A frequent critique of Hegel's idea of the whole, especially coming from the postmodern camp, is that it dominates the individual elements as a totality, and thus represses their plurality and heterogeneity. However, this critique does not do justice to Hegel's idea of the whole or of the concept. Hegel's whole is not a structure of domination, no totality subjugating and enslaving its parts. Rather, it opens up the parts' space for moving and acting in the first place, and thus makes freedom possible: 'The whole is . . . the One which contains bound within itself the parts in their freedom.'[4] The whole is a figure of mediation and reconciliation, a harmonious unity, a 'stable equilibrium of all parts'.[5] The whole is reconciling. The concept founds a unity 'in which the separate sides and their opposition persist in no real independence and fixity over against one another but count still as only ideal factors reconciled into a free harmony'.[6] Reconciliation is the task of philosophy as such:

[P]hilosophy enters into the heart of the self-contradictory characteristics, knows them in their essential nature, i.e. as in their one-sidedness not absolute but self-dissolving, and it sets them in the harmony and unity which is truth.[7]

Truth is reconciliation. Truth is freedom.

The concept brings forth a harmonious whole. What is beautiful is the non-coercive agreement of the parts in a whole:

> In the beautiful object there must be both (i) necessity, established by the Concept, in the coherence of its particular aspects, and (ii) the appearance of their freedom, freedom for themselves and not merely for the unity of the parts on view.[8]

Constitutive of beauty is the freedom of the parts *for themselves* within a unity or whole.

The beautiful object is something over against the subject, something with which the subject develops a *free* relationship. The subject is not free in relation to an object as long as it is either dependent on it, or wants to impose his or her will, purpose, or interests on it, and thus encounters its resistance. The aesthetic takes up a position *in the middle and as mediating* between the *theoretical* and the *practical*:

> In the field of *theory* the *subject* is finite and unfree because the independence of things is presupposed; the same is true in the field of *practice*, owing to the one-sidedness, struggle, and inner contradiction between aims and the

impulses and passions aroused from outside, and owing also to the never wholly eliminated resistance of the objects.[9]

In the theoretical realm, the subject is not free because of the independence of things. In the practical realm, the subject is also not free because it subjugates the things to its impulses and passions. Here, it is confronted with the resistance coming from the things. Only in the *aesthetic* relation with the object is the subject finally free. The aesthetic relationship also releases the object into its specificity. The artistic object is characterized by freedom and the absence of compulsion. The aesthetic relation does not exert any pressure on the object at all, does not impose anything on it that would be external to it. Art is a practice of freedom and reconciliation:

> From the practical interest of desire, the interest of art is distinguished by the fact that it lets its object persist freely and on its own account, while desire converts it to its own use by destroying it. On the other hand, the consideration of art differs in an opposite way from theoretical consideration by scientific intelligence, since it cherishes an interest in the object in its individual existence and does not struggle to change it into its universal thought and concept.[10]

The beautiful object is an object over against the subject, in which any kind of dependence and compulsion has disappeared. As a pure end in itself it is free of any determination from outside, 'in which it served purposes external to it as a useful means of fulfilling them, and either, unfree, armed itself against their fulfilment or else was compelled to accept the alien purpose as its own'.[11] The beautiful object is neither 'forced' nor 'compelled by us'.[12] In the face of the beautiful as the 'perfectly realized Concept and end',[13] the *subject, by itself,* entirely relinquishes its interest in it. The subject's 'desire' steps back.[14] The subject does not try to instrumentalize the beautiful object for its own purposes; it 'cancels his aims in relation to the object and treats it as independent, an end in itself'.[15] *Letting be [Seinlassen],* even *releasement [Gelassenheit]* would be the subject's attitude towards the beautiful. Only beauty teaches *disinterested lingering*:

> Thus the contemplation of beauty is of a liberal kind; it leaves objects alone as being inherently free and infinite; there is no wish to possess them or take advantage of them as useful for fulfilling finite needs and intentions.[16]

In the face of beauty, the separation of subject and object, of ego and thing [*Gegenstand*], also disappears. In *contemplating* the object, the subject becomes *immersed* in the object and unites, reconciles itself with it:

> But the self in relation to the object likewise ceases to be the abstraction of both noticing, sensuously perceiving, and observing, ... In this [beautiful] object the self becomes concrete in itself since it makes explicit the unity of Concept and reality, the unification, in their concreteness, of the aspects hitherto separated, and therefore abstract, in the self and its object.[17]

Hegel's aesthetic of beauty is an aesthetic of truth and freedom, which withdraws beauty from any form of consumption. Neither 'truth' nor the 'concept' can be consumed. Beauty is an end in itself. Its brilliance concerns itself, its inner necessity. It does not submit itself to any *in order to*, any external context of use, because it exists for its own sake. Beauty rests in itself. For Hegel, no object of daily use, no object of consumption, no commodity would be beautiful. They lack the inner independence and freedom which account for beauty. Consumption and beauty are mutually exclusive. Beauty does not *promote* itself. It does not tempt you to enjoy or to possess it. Rather, it invites you to linger in contemplation. It lets desire as well as interest disappear. Thus, art does not agree with capitalism which subjects everything to consumption and speculation.

Truth is the counter-figure to the 'aggregate' [*Haufen*]. There is no such thing as an *aggregate of truth* [*Wahrheitshaufen*]. Truth, therefore, does not appear *often* [*häufig*]. Like beauty, truth is a form, while an aggregate is formless. Hegel does not see 'baroque connections' as beautiful because they form a heap, an unconnected, and that means non-conceptual, side-by-side.[18] The things in a heap are coupled with each other despite their conceptual distance. The baroque lacks the tendency towards the One, namely the concept, which constitutes beauty.

Truth reduces *entropy*, namely the *level of noise*. Without truth, without concepts, reality disintegrates into a noisy heap. Beauty as well as truth is something *exclusive*. Thus they do not occur *often* [*häufig*]. A *creative exclusion* is proper to them. *Theory* also provides this. Although useful information may be distilled out of the heap of

56

data that is Big Data, this generates neither *knowledge* nor *truth*. The 'end of theory', invoked by Chris Anderson as a result of the complete substitution of theory with data,[19] would mean the end of truth, the end of narration, the end of spirit. Data is purely *additive*. Addition is opposed to narration. A verticality is inherent to truth. Data and information, by contrast, inhabit a horizontal space.

Beauty promises freedom and reconciliation. In the face of beauty, desire and compulsion disappear. Thus, it makes possible a free relationship with the world and with oneself. Hegel's aesthetics of beauty is diametrically opposed to today's *kalocracy*. The neoliberal rule of beauty produces compulsions. Botox, bulimia and cosmetic surgery reflect its terror. The task of beauty, first of all, is to produce stimuli and to generate attention. Even art, for Hegel *inalienable*, is today entirely subjected to the logic of capital. The freedom of art submits itself to the freedom of capital.

10

The Politics of Beauty

In his *Anthropology from a Pragmatic Point of View*, Kant understands 'wit' (*ingenium*) as 'a kind of intellectual luxury'.[1] Wit becomes possible in a space of freedom that is liberated from needs and necessity. That is why it is '*blooming*', 'just as nature seems to be carrying on more of a game with its flowers but a business with fruits'.[2] The beauty of flowers is owed to a *luxury* which is free of any economic aspect. It is the expression of a free *play* without compulsions and needs. Thus, it is opposed to *work* and *business*. Where compulsion and needs reign, there are no free spaces for the element of play which is constitutive of beauty. Beauty is a phenomenon of luxury. The necessary [*Notwendige*] which only averts [*wendet*] needs [*Not*] is not beautiful.

For Aristotle, the free man is someone who is independent of the needs of life and its compulsions. Such a person has three forms of life at his disposal. They are distinct from those forms of life which purely serve the preservation of life. Thus, the life of the merchant, which is only aimed at making gains, is not free: 'The remaining three ways of life have in common that they were concerned with the "beautiful", that is, with things neither necessary nor merely useful.'[3] These are a life devoted to the enjoyment of beautiful things; a life which produces beautiful deeds in the polis; and, finally, the contemplative life of the philosopher, which is spent in the realm of everlasting beauty by investigating that which never perishes.

Acting is what constitutes the life of the politician (*bios politikos*). He is not subject to the verdict of necessity and utility. Neither labouring nor producing makes a *bios politikos*. As these only produce what is necessary and useful for sustaining life, they are not among the forms of life worthy of a free man, those in which freedom manifests itself. They do not take place *for their own sake*. Because they are unfree and externally determined, they are not beautiful. As social organizations are necessary for communal living, they do not represent genuinely political activity. Neither necessity nor utility are categories pertaining to beauty. As free individuals, politicians must create beautiful deeds beyond what is necessary and useful for pure sustenance. Political action consists in the creation of entirely new beginnings.

Any kind of compulsion or necessity deprives acting of its beauty. Those things or activities are beautiful which are not dominated by necessity and utility. The forms of life of the free person are all *luxury* insofar as they *luxate*, that is *deviate*. The actions belonging to the household or

59

administration, which are necessary for the preservation of a community, are not genuinely political actions.

In both Plato and Aristotle, the beautiful (*to kalon*) far exceeds the realm of aesthetic sensibility. Aristotle's ethics of happiness (*eudaimonia*) proves to be an *ethics of beauty*. The striving for justice is also motivated by its beauty. Plato counts it among the most beautiful things (*to kalliston*).[4] In his *Eudemian Ethics*, Aristotle introduces the idiosyncratic concept of *kalokagathia*, the '*beautiful-good*'.[5] The good is here subordinated to the beautiful; it takes second place. The good is realized in the brilliance of the beautiful. The ideal politics is a *politics of beauty*.

At present, such a *politics of beauty* is impossible because all of politics today is subject to systemic pressures. It possesses hardly any free spaces. The politics of beauty is a politics of freedom. The *absence of alternatives*, which is the yoke under which today's politics *works*, makes genuine political action impossible. Politics does not *act*; it *works*. Politics would need to offer genuine alternatives, a real *choice* [*Wahl*].[6] Otherwise it degenerates into a dictatorship. A politician who is a stooge of the system is not a free man in the Aristotelian sense, but a servant.

The English word 'fair' is characterized by its multidimensionality. It means 'just' as well as 'beautiful'. The Old High German *fagar* also means beautiful. The German word '*fegen*' [to sweep] originally meant 'to render brilliant'. The double meaning of 'fair' is a striking indication that beauty and justice originally derive from the same idea. Justice is felt to be beautiful. Justice and beauty have a special *synaesthetic* connection.

In her book *On Beauty and Being Just*, Elaine Scarry describes the ethical and political implications of beauty, and tries to find an aesthetic approach to ethical experience. The perception of beauty, or the presence of beauty, she writes, implies an 'invitation to ethical fairness'.[7] Certain characteristics of beauty sharpen the intuitive sense of justice: 'We have seen how the beautiful object . . . assists in turning us to justice.'[8] Symmetry, which is also the basis of the idea of justice, is beautiful. A just relation necessarily entails a symmetric relation. Total asymmetry produces a sensation of ugliness. Injustice finds expression as an extremely asymmetric relation. Plato conceives of the good from the perspective of symmetry's beauty.

Scarry points to an experience of beauty which makes the subject *less narcissistic*, even *less inwardly orientated*. Faced with beauty, the subject abdicates. This leaves room for the other. This radical retraction of the self in favour of the other is an ethical act:

> Beauty, according to [Simone] Weil, requires us 'to give up our imaginary position at the center.' . . . It is not that we cease to stand at the center of the world, for we never stood there. It is that we cease to stand even at the center of our own world. We willingly cede our ground to the thing that stands before us.[9]

In the face of beauty, the subject takes a side (*lateral*) position; it steps aside instead of pushing to the fore. It becomes a *lateral figure*. It takes itself back in favour of the other. This aesthetic experience in the face of beauty, Scarry believes, extends into the ethical. The retraction of the self is essential to justice. Thus, justice is a *beautiful* state of being together. Aesthetic joy can be translated

61

into the ethical realm: 'It is clear that an *ethical fairness* which requires "a symmetry of everyone's relation" will be greatly assisted by an *aesthetic fairness* that creates in all participants a state of delight in their own lateralness.'[10]

Contrary to Scarry's expectation, the experience of beauty today is fundamentally narcissistic. It is dominated not by a *lateralness*, but by a narcissistic *centralness*.[11] It becomes consumerist. Towards the object of consumption one takes up a *central* position. This consumerist attitude destroys the *otherness of the other* in favour of which one would *step aside* or *step down*. It destroys the *otherness of the other*, *alterity*.

Sexiness is also incompatible with fairness. It does not allow for any lateralness. Today, the kind of experience of beauty that would shake the central position of the subject is impossible. Beauty itself becomes pornographic, even *anaesthetic*. It loses all *transcendence*, all *significance*, even all *valency*, that would allow it to exceed the merely aesthetic and to link up with the ethical and the political. Wholly de-coupled from the ethical and moral power of judgement, beauty hands itself over to the *immanence of consumption*.

11

Pornographic Theatre

Asked why he retired from the world of theatre for good, Botho Strauß answered:

> But it is simply all over. I wanted to be an erotic author for the stage, but today pornographic authors – pornographic in the aesthetic or literal sense – dominate the theatres. I am interested in erotic connections and vicissitudes, but today connections and changes are no longer shown; all that is ever put on display is the pornographic side of things . . .[1]

An eroticist differs from a pornographer by being indirect and circuitous. An eroticist loves *scenic distance*, and is content with making allusions instead of putting things openly on display. An erotic actor is not a pornographic exhibitor. Eroticism is *allusive*, not *affective*. In this way it is distinct from pornography. *Straight on* is the temporal modality of pornography. Delays, slowing down and distraction are temporal modalities of the erotic. *Deixis*, the direct pointing at a matter, is pornographic. Pornography avoids detours. It gets straight down to business. Erotic, by contrast, are signs which *circulate* without disclosing themselves. Pornographic theatre is the theatre of disclosure. Erotic are secrets that, in principle, *cannot be disclosed*. This is how they differ from *hidden, withheld information* that could, in principle, be disclosed. Pornographic is precisely the progressive disclosure down to the *truth* or *transparency*.

Pornographic theatre lacks dialogue. It is, says Strauß, an 'undertaking of private psychopathy'. The capacity for dialogue, the capacity for opening up to the other, even the capacity for *listening*, is today diminishing on all levels. The contemporary narcissistic subject perceives everything as nothing but shades of itself. It is incapable of seeing the otherness of the other. A dialogue is not a staging of mutual exposure. Neither confessions nor disclosures are erotic.

In a laudatory speech for Jutta Lampe, Botho Strauß writes:

Whereas a moment ago, we still heard the silvery, almost singing tone of a girl, the next moment it is abruptly lowered by an interval and becomes a guttural, almost blaring, at times downright vulgar sound. This fast-changing pitch of the voice is not a gesture of coloratura, but expresses a strong dialogic commitment, the wish to learn something of the other at all cost, and together with him.[2]

A weakness of dialogic commitment characterizes today's society. Where dialogue disappears from the stage, a theatre of affectivity emerges. Affects are not dialogically structured. A *negation of the other* is inscribed in them.

Feelings [*Gefühle*] are narrative. Emotions [*Emotionen*] are impulsive. Neither emotions nor affects open up a narrative space. Affective theatre does not *narrate*. Rather, a mass of affects is loaded directly on to the stage. This is what constitutes its pornographic character.

Feelings also have a different temporality from that of emotions and affects. They possess duration, a narrative length. Emotions are much more volatile than feelings. Affects are limited to the moment. And only feelings have access to dialogue, to the *other*. This is why there is such a thing as compassion [*Mitgefühl*]. Com-emotions, or com-affects, by contrast, do not exist. Affects as well as emotions are forms of expressions belonging to isolated, monological subjects.

Today's society of intimacy removes more and more objective forms of play and the room for play in which one could escape *oneself*, one's own *psychology*. Intimacy is opposed to playful distance and theatricality. Objective forms are decisive in playing, not subjective, psychological states. Strict play or rituals unburden the soul. They do not allow for any space to be given to a pornography of the soul: 'Eccentricity, egomania, exaltation are not to be found here. Grace and strict play rule out emotional caprice, nudism of the soul, and anything psychopathic.' The actress [*Schauspielerin*], the passionate *player* [*Spielerin*], is *de-psychologized, de-subjectified and freed of all inwardness*, and becomes a *nobody*: 'You are a Nobody, else you would not be a great actress.' A *Nobody* (Latin: *nemo*)

65

does not have a soul that could be exposed. Against the pornographic nudism of the soul, against all psychopathy, Strauß calls for a *nemological self-transparency* in which one exceeds oneself, moves towards, and allows oneself to be seduced by, the other. Erotic theatre is the place where such seduction, the *phantasy for the other*, is possible.

12

Lingering on Beauty

Faust's invocation 'If ever I shall tell the moment:/Bide here, you are so beautiful' conceals an important aspect of beauty.[1] Beauty itself actually invites us to linger; it is the will which stands in the way of contemplative lingering. But at the sight of beauty, willing retreats. This contemplative side of beauty is central to Schopenhauer's understanding of art according to which

> . . . aesthetic pleasure in the beautiful consists, to a large extent, in the fact that, when we enter the state of pure contemplation, we are raised for the moment above all willing, above all desires and cares; we are, so to speak, rid of ourselves.[2]

Beauty frees me from myself. The ego immerses itself in beauty. It *rids itself* of itself in the face of beauty. It is the *willing*, the *interest*, even the *conatus* (the *striving*), which make time pass. The contemplative immersion in beauty, in which willing retreats and the self withdraws, produces a state in which time, so to speak, is at a stand-*still*. The absence of willing and interest brings time to a stand-*still*, even renders it *still*. *Stillness* is what distinguishes aesthetic intuition from mere sensual perception. In the face of beauty, seeing *comes into its own* [*kommt an*]. It no longer is driven away, torn away. This *coming into its own* [*Ankunft*] is essential for beauty.

The 'presence-eternity' of a lingering which overcomes time, aims at the *other*:

> It [the presence-eternity] is the presence of the other. Thus, in lingering eternity begins to shine as a light that spreads across the other. If it has ever been considered in the philosophical tradition at all, then in Spinoza's sentence: 'The mind is eternal to the extent that it grasps the things from the perspective of eternity.'

It follows that the task of art is the *saving of the other*. *The saving of beauty is the saving of the other*. Art saves the *other* by 'resisting its identification with its givenness [*Vorhandenheit*]'.[3] Beauty as that which is *wholly other* suspends the *violence of time*. The crisis of beauty today consists precisely in the fact that beauty is reduced to its givenness, to its use or consumer value. Consumption destroys the *other*. The *beauty of art* is a form of resistance to it.

For Nietzsche, original art is the art of the festival. Works of art are testimonies to those blissful moments in the life of a culture in which the *passing* of ordinary time is suspended:

What do all our art of artworks matter if we lose that higher art, the art of festivals! Formerly, all artworks were displayed on the great festival road of humanity, as commemorations and memorials of high and happy moments. Now one uses artworks to lure poor, exhausted, and sick human beings to the side of humanity's road of suffering for a short lascivious moment; one offers them a little intoxication and madness.[4]

Works of art are monuments of the heydays [*der Hochzeit*],[5] even of the high-times [*Hoch-Zeit*], in which ordinary time suspends itself. The festive time as high-time brings the time of everyday life, the ordinary time for work, to a stand*still*. The brilliance of eternity is inherent to festive time. If the 'festival road' is replaced with the 'road of suffering', the heydays are degraded to a 'short lascivious moment' with 'a little intoxication'.

Festivals as well as celebrations have religious origins. The Latin *feriae* refers to the time dedicated to religious and cult practices. *Fanum* means a holy place consecrated to a divinity. The festival begins where the pro-fane ordinary time (literally: the time before the holy district) ends. It presupposes a consecration. At the high-time of the festival, one is initiated. If this threshold, this transition, this consecration, which separates the holy and the pro-fane, is suspended, all that remains is ordinary, transient time, which is then exploited as time for work. Today, the high-time has disappeared altogether in favour of the time for work which has become total. Even breaks are integrated into working hours. They are only short interruptions of the working hours, in which one re-creates in order to put oneself at the full disposal of the working process again. Breaks are not the other of working hours. Thus, they do not improve the quality of time.

In his essay on 'The Relevance of the Beautiful', Gadamer establishes a connection between art and the festival. He begins by pointing out the linguistic specificity that 'we speak of enacting a celebration'.[6] This enacting [Begehen] points towards the specific temporality of a festival:

> The word 'enacting' removes all idea of a goal to be attained. To enact is not to set out in order subsequently to arrive somewhere, for when we enact a festival, then the festival is always there from the beginning. The temporal character of the festive celebration that we enact lies in the fact that it does not dissolve into a series of separate moments.[7]

During a festival, another time reigns. Time as a *succession* of transient, fleeting moments is suspended. There is no goal that one would have to reach. It is precisely the reaching [Hingehen] which makes time pass [vergehen]. *The enacting [Begehen] of a festival suspends the passing [Vergehen]*. Something everlasting is intrinsic to a festival, to a festive high-time. An analogy exists between art and festival: 'The essence of our temporal experience of art is in learning how to tarry in this way. And perhaps it is the only way that is granted to us finite beings to relate to what we call eternity.'[8]

Works of art lose their cult value the moment they are exhibited. Their value as objects to be exhibited replaces their cult value. The works of art are no longer displayed on the festival road, but in museums. Exhibitions are not

70

festivals, but spectacles. The museum is their Golgotha [*Schädelstätte*]. Here, things only acquire a value if they are seen, if they meet with attention, while cult objects often remain hidden. Their hiddenness even increases their cult value. A cult has nothing to do with attention. The totalization of attention destroys the cultic.

Today, works of art are primarily traded on the market and stock-market road. They have neither cult value, nor value as exhibition pieces. Rather, it is purely their value as objects of speculation which subjects them to the logic of capital. Today, value as object of speculation turns out to be the supreme value. The stock exchange is today's place of worship. Total revenue [*absoluter Erlös*] takes the place of salvation [*Erlösung*].

13

Beauty as Reminiscence

Walter Benjamin raises recollection to the status of the essence of human existence. It is the source of 'all the power of internalized existence'. It also accounts for the essence of beauty. Even amidst beauty's 'blossoming', it remains 'inessential' [*wesenlos*] without recollection. Essential to beauty is not the presence of immediate brilliance, but the *past* of a recollection and its afterglow. Thus, Benjamin appeals to Plato:

> The words of Plato's 'Phaedrus' testify to this: 'But when one is fresh from the mystery and who saw much of the vision beholds a godlike face or bodily form that truly expresses beauty, he is at first seized with shuddering and a measure of that awe which the vision inspired, then with reverence as if at the sight of a god; ... At this sight, his memory returns to that form of beauty, and he

sees her once again enthroned by the side of temperance upon her holy seat.'[1]

Faced with a beautiful form, one is reminded of the *past*. For Plato, the experience of beauty is a repetition of the past, a *re-cognition*.

The experience of beauty as a recollection evades consumption, which is dominated by an entirely different kind of temporality. What is consumed is always the *new*, and not the *past*. Re-cognition would even be detrimental to consumption. The temporality of consumption is not a *having been* [*Gewesenheit*]. Recollections and duration are not compatible with consumption. Consumption lives off splintered time. It destroys duration in the interest of maximization. The flood of information, the rapid cutting sequences, which force the eye quickly to digest what it sees, also do not allow for lingering recollection. Digital images cannot attract attention in lasting fashion. They quickly eject their visual stimuli and fade away.

Marcel Proust's key experience is the experience of duration triggered by the taste of the madeleine dipped in lime-blossom tea. It is a moment of recollection. A 'tiny' drop of tea expands into a 'vast structure of recollection'.[2] Proust is afforded a small 'fragment of time in the pure state'.[3] Time is compressed into a fragrant crystal of time, into a 'vase full of scents'.[4] This liberates Proust from the fleetingness of time:

An exquisite pleasure had invaded my senses, something isolated, detached, with no suggestion of its origin. And at once the vicissitudes of life had become indifferent to me, its disasters innocuous, its brevity illusory – this new

73

sensation having had the effect, which love has, of filling me with a precious essence; or rather this essence was not in me, it *was* me. I had ceased now to feel mediocre, contingent, mortal.[5]

Proust's narration practises a temporality which founds duration within an 'age of haste' in which everything, even art, is 'brief'.[6] Proust's narration opposes the 'simple cinematographic vision'[7] and cinematographic time which disintegrates into a quick succession of point-like presences. The exhilarating experience of duration emerges from a blending of past and present. The present is touched, enlivened, even fertilized, by recollection:

And this cause I began to divine as I compared these diverse happy impressions, diverse yet with this in common, that I experienced them at the present moment and at the same time in the context of a distant moment, so that the past was made to encroach upon the present and I was made to doubt whether I was in the one or the other.[8]

It is not the immediate presence and contiguity of things that is beautiful. Essential to beauty are rather the secret correspondences between things and ideas that take place across vast spaces of time. Proust believes that life itself represents a network of relations, 'perpetually weaving fresh threads which link one individual and one event to another', and that these threads are 'doubled and redoubled' by life 'to thicken the web, so that between any slightest point of our past and all the others a rich network of memories gives us an almost infinite variety of communicating paths to choose from'.[9] Beauty occurs where things turn towards each other and enter into relations with each other. It *narrates*. Like truth, it is a *narrative* event:

> . . . truth will be attained by him [the author] only when he takes two different objects, states the connexion between them . . . and encloses them in the necessary links of a well-wrought style; truth – and life too – can be attained by us only when, by comparing a quality common to two sensations, we succeed in extracting their common essence and in reuniting them to each other, liberated from the contingencies of time, within a metaphor[, thus linking them to each other through the ineffable efficacy of the combination of words].[10]

The 'Internet of Things', which connects objects with each other, does not have a narrative nature. Communication as the exchange of information does not *recount* anything. It only *counts*. Narrative links, by contrast, are beautiful. Today, addition pushes aside narration. Narrative relations give way to informational connections. The amassing of information does not yield a narration. Metaphors are narrative relations. They let things and events enter into a conversation with each other.

The task of the writer is to metaphorize, that is to poeticize, the world. The writer's poetic perspective discovers the hidden liaisons between things. Beauty is a relational event. A specific temporality is inherent to it. It evades being enjoyed immediately because the beauty of a thing only appears much later in the light of another, as a *reminiscence*. It consists of historical layers which emit a phosphorescent glow.

Beauty is something *hesitating*, a *latecomer*. Not the present brilliance, but the still afterglow is beautiful. This reserve accounts for its nobleness. Immediate stimuli and excitations block the access to beauty. The things only unveil their hidden beauty, their fragrant essence, belatedly via detours. Long-lasting and slow: that is the pace of beauty. One does not happen across beauty in an immediate encounter. Rather, it occurs in the form of a renewed encounter and a re-cognition:

> The slow arrow of beauty. The most noble kind of beauty is that which does not carry us away suddenly, whose attacks are not violent or intoxicating (this kind easily awakens disgust), but rather the kind of beauty which infiltrates slowly, which we carry along with us almost unnoticed, and meet up with again in dreams . . .[11]

14

Giving Birth in Beauty

A rumbling: truth
itself has appeared
among humankind
in the very thick of their flurrying metaphors.

Paul Celan[1]

In the *Symposium*, Plato sets up a gradation of beauty. The lover of beauty is not content with the view of a beautiful body. He or she moves up the ladder beyond ordinary beauty to the point of beauty as such. However, the inclination towards beautiful bodies is not condemned. Rather, it is an essential part, even the necessary initial point, of the ascent towards beauty.

The specificity of Plato's theory of beauty is that the attitude towards beauty is not passive and consumptive, but active and generative. Faced with beauty, the soul is driven to create something beautiful itself. When viewing beauty, Eros awakens a procreative capacity in the soul. Thus, he calls it 'giving birth in beauty' [*tokos en kalo*].[2]

Through beauty, Eros has access to what is immortal. The 'immortal children' begotten by him are works (*erga*), not just poetic or philosophical works, but also political works. Thus, Plato praises the works of poets like Homer or Hesiod, as well as those of rulers such as Solon or Lycurgus. Beautiful laws are the work of Eros. It is not only philosophers or poets who are eroticists, but also politicians. Beautiful political deeds, like philosophical works, owe their origin to Eros. A politics that is guided by Eros is a *politics of beauty*.

As a deity, Eros consecrates thinking. Socrates is initiated to the 'mysteries of Eros' by Diotima. These mysteries escape both knowledge (*episteme*) and speech (*logos*). Heidegger was an eroticist, too. According to him, it is Eros who gives wings to thought and guides it:

> I call it Eros, the oldest of the gods according to Parmenides. . . . The beat of that god's wings moves me each time I take a substantial step in my thinking and venture onto untrodden paths.[3]

Without the participation of Eros, thinking is degraded to 'pure work'. Work, which is opposed to Eros, desecrates and disenchants thinking.

The place of beauty, according to Heidegger, is not in the aesthetic but in the ontological realm. He is a Platonist. Beauty, Heidegger says, is the 'poetic name for being'.[4] Eros is directed at being: 'But being is understood in striving for being, or, as the Greeks say, in

78

ἔρως.'⁵ Beauty is given an ontological consecration. The 'ontological difference' distinguishes being from beings. Beings are all that *is*. But it owes its meaning to being. Being is not the ground from which beings emerge but the horizon of sense and understanding in the light of which an understanding *self-comportment* towards beings becomes possible in the first place.

Heidegger explicitly understands the beautiful as a phenomenon of truth beyond aesthetic pleasure:

> Truth is the truth of being. Beauty does not occur apart from this truth. It appears when truth sets itself into the work. This appearing (as this being of truth in the work and as the work) is beauty. Thus beauty belongs to the advent of truth. It does not exist merely relative to pleasure, and purely as its object.⁶

Truth, as the truth of being, is a process, an event, which confers meaning and significance on to beings in the first place. Thus, a new truth lets beings appear in an altogether different light, and changes our relationship with the world, our understanding of reality. It lets everything appear differently. The advent of truth defines anew what *is* real. It brings forth *another Is*. The work is the place which receives and embodies the advent of truth. Eros is inclined towards the beautiful, the appearance of truth. This is where he differs from *pleasure*. A time in which pleasure, the *Like*, is predominant, Heidegger would say, is a *time without Eros, without beauty*.

Beauty, as the advent of truth, is *generative*, creative, even *poetic*. It *gives* something to see. This given *gift* is beautiful. The work is not beautiful as a product but as

79

the *shining through* of truth. Beauty also transcends *disinterested pleasure*. The aesthetic has no access to beauty in the emphatic sense. Beauty as the shining through [*Hervorscheinen*] of truth is inconspicuous [*unscheinbar*] insofar as it hides behind the phenomena [*Erscheinungen*]. In Plato, too, it is necessary to ignore beautiful forms to a certain extent in order to become capable of seeing *beauty as such*.

Today, all consecration is taken away from beauty. It is no longer an occurrence of truth. No ontological difference and no Eros protects beauty against consumption. It is *merely one of the beings*, something that is simply given and present in its ordinariness. One simply comes across it as an object causing immediate pleasure. The *giving birth in beauty* gives way to beauty as a product, as an object for consumption and aesthetic pleasure.

The beautiful is what commits us [*das Verbindliche*]. It founds duration. It is no coincidence that beauty 'itself by itself with itself',[7] in Plato, 'always is and neither comes to be nor passes away'.[8] It is what commits us, what gives the measure, the *gift* of measure [*Maß-Gabe*] as such. Eros means *striving for what is binding*. Badiou would call it 'fidelity'. In his *In Praise of Love*, he writes:

But what they are always saying is: I shall extract something else from what was mere chance. I'm going to extract something that will endure, something that will persist, a commitment, a fidelity. And here I am using the word 'fidelity' within my own philosophical jargon, stripped of its usual connotations. It means precisely that transition from random encounter to a construction that is resilient, as if it had been necessary.[9]

80

Fidelity and what commits us are mutually dependent. Commitment demands fidelity. Fidelity presupposes commitment. Fidelity is *unconditional*. This is what constitutes its *metaphysics*, its *transcendence* even. The increasing aestheticization of everyday life renders especially the experience of beauty, as the experience of what commits us, impossible. It only produces objects for our fleeting pleasure. The increasing volatility not only concerns the financial markets. At present, it takes hold of society as a whole. Nothing lasts or endures. The radical contingency awakens a longing for something that commits us, something beyond the ordinary. Today, we are faced with a *crisis of beauty* insofar as the beautiful is smoothened out into objects of pleasure, of the *Like*, into something arbitrary and comfortable. The saving of beauty is the saving of that which commits us.

Notes

Epigraph, p.vi

1 Untitled poem from *Atemwende* [*Breathturn*], in Paul Celan, *Selected Poems*, transl. Michael Hamburger (London: Penguin, 1996), p. 279.

Chapter 1. The Smooth

1 Georg Wilhelm Friedrich Hegel, *Aesthetics: Lectures on Fine Art*, vol.1, transl. T. M. Knox (Oxford: Clarendon Press, 1975), p. 38.

2 Ibid., p. 39.

3 Ibid., pp. 38f.

4 Roland Barthes, *Mythologies*, transl. Annette Lavers (London: Vintage, 1993), pp. 88f.

5 Ibid., p. 90.

6 Christian Gampert on the *Kultur heute* [Culture today] programme, Deutschlandfunk, 14 May 2012.

7 'Jeff Koons über Vertrauen' [Jeff Koons on trust], *Süddeutsche Zeitung*, 17 May 2010.

8 Hans-Georg Gadamer, 'The Relevance of the Beautiful', transl. Robert Bernasconi and Nick Walker, in *The Relevance of the Beautiful and other Essays* (Cambridge: Cambridge University Press, 1987), pp. 1–55; here p. 34.

9 Cf. Wolfgang Welsch, *Ästhetisches Denken* (Stuttgart: Reclam, 2010), pp. 9ff. Welsch interprets anaestheticization, or anaesthetics, not as anaesthesia, but as non-aesthetics, and tries to find positive aspects in it.

10 Roland Barthes, *The Pleasure of the Text*, transl. Richard Miller (New York: Hill and Wang, 1975), p. 10.

11 Jean Baudrillard, *Das Andere selbst* (Vienna: Edition Passagen, 1994), p. 27.

12 Georges Bataille, *Eroticism*, transl. Mary Dalwood (San Francisco, CA: City Lights Books, 1986), p. 145.

13 Winfried Menninghaus, *Disgust: The Theory and History of a Strong Sensation*, transl. Howard Eiland and Joel Golb (New York: SUNY Press, 2003), p. 1.

14 Karl Rosenkranz, *The Aesthetics of Ugliness*, transl. Andrei Pop and Mechtild Widrich (London/New York: Bloomsbury, 2015), p. 190f.

15 Transl. note: *Jungle Camp*, the German equivalent to *I'm a Celebrity . . . Get Me Out of Here!*

16 Robert Pfaller, *Das schmutzige Heilige und die reine Vernunft: Symptome der Gegenwartskultur* (Frankfurt/M.: S. Fischer, 2008), p. 11.

Chapter 2. The Smooth Body

1 Jean Baudrillard, *Das Andere selbst* (Vienna: Edition Passagen, 1994), p. 27.

2 Walter Benjamin, *The Work of Art in the Age of Its*

Technological Reproducibility (second version), in *The Work of Art in the Age of Its Technological Reproducibility and Other Writings on Media*, transl. Edmund Jephcott and Harry Zohn (Cambridge, MA, and London: Belknap Press, 2008), pp. 19–55; here p. 37.

3 Roland Barthes, *Camera Lucida*, transl. Richard Howard (New York: Farrar, Straus & Giroux, 1999), p. 113.

4 Transl. note: The mission of the Quantified Self movement, according to its website, is 'to support new discoveries about ourselves and our communities that are grounded in accurate observation and enlivened by a spirit of friendship'. It is coordinated by 'Quantified Self Labs', a 'California-based company founded by Gary Wolf and Kevin Kelly that serves the Quantified Self user community worldwide by producing international meetings, conferences and expositions, community forums, web content and services, and a guide to self-tracking tools'; available at: <http://quantifiedself.com/about/>.

5 Transl. note: 'Car-sharing' and 'sharing', here and below, in English in the original.

Chapter 3. The Aesthetics of the Smooth

1 Plato, *Symposium*, transl. Alexander Nehamas and Paul Woodruff, in *Complete Works* (Indianapolis, IN, and Cambridge: Hackett, 1997), pp. 457–505; here p. 493 (210e).

2 Ibid., p. 494 (211e).

3 Plato, *Phaidros*, transl. Alexander Nehamas and Paul Woodruff, in *Complete Works* (Indianapolis, IN, and Cambridge: Hackett, 1997), pp. 506–56; here p. 522 (244a).

4 Edmund Burke, *A Philosophical Enquiry into the Origin of Our Ideas of the Sublime and Beautiful* (Oxford: Oxford University Press, 2015), p. 121.

84

5 Ibid., p. 93.

6 Ibid., p. 97.

7 Ibid.

8 Ibid., p. 120.

9 Ibid., p. 92.

10 Ibid.

11 Ibid., p. 93.

12 Ibid., p. 121.

13 Ibid., p. 109.

14 Ibid.

15 Immanuel Kant, *Critique of the Power of Judgment*, transl. Paul Guyer and Eric Matthews (Cambridge: Cambridge University Press, 2002), p. 103.

16 Ibid., p. 122.

17 Ibid., p. 104.

18 Theodor W. Adorno, *Aesthetic Theory*, transl. Robert Hullot-Kentor (London and New York: Continuum, 1997), p. 48.

19 Immanuel Kant, *Critique of the Power of Judgment*, p. 145.

20 Ibid., p. 145.

21 Ibid., pp. 128f.

22 Ibid., p. 129.

23 Ibid., p. 141.

24 Ibid., p. 129.

25 Ibid., p. 151.

26 As does, for instance, Wolfgang Welsch, *Ästhetisches Denken* (Stuttgart: Reclam, 2003).

Chapter 4. Digital Beauty

1 Theodor W. Adorno, *Aesthetic Theory*, transl. Robert Hullot-Kentor (London and New York: Continuum, 1997), p. 276.

2 Ibid.
3 Ibid., p. 245.
4 Ibid., p. 69.
5 Ibid., p. 73.
6 Ibid., pp. 70f.
7 Ibid., p. 74.
8 Ibid., p. 73.
9 Ibid., p. 74.
10 Ibid., p. 72.
11 Ibid.
12 Ibid., p. 73.
13 Ibid., p. 74.
14 Ibid., p. 73.

Chapter 5. The Aesthetics of Veiling

1 Roland Barthes, *Camera Lucida*, transl. Richard Howard (New York: Farrar, Straus & Giroux, 1999), p. 41.
2 Ibid., pp. 41f.
3 Walter Benjamin, 'Goethe's Elective Affinities', transl. Stanley Corngold, in *Selected Writings*, vol. 1 (1913–1926) (Cambridge, MA, and London: Harvard University Press, 1996), pp. 297–560; here p. 352.
4 Johann Wolfgang Goethe, *Faust: Part II*, transl. David Constantine (London: Penguin, 2005), pp. 182f. (lines 9945–50). [David Constantine's translation has here been substituted for the one in *Selected Writings*.]
5 Ibid., p. 351.
6 Ibid.
7 Saint Augustine, *On Christian Doctrine*, transl. James F. Shaw (no place: CreateSpace, 2015), p. 238. [Transl. note: The passage in question discusses St Paul's qualities as an orator.]

8 Gershom Scholem, *On the Kabbalah and Its Symbolism*, transl. Ralph Manheim (New York: Schocken Books, 1969), p. 55.

9 Ibid.

10 Ibid., p. 56.

11 Roland Barthes, *The Pleasure of the Text*, p. 9.

12 Ibid., p. 10.

13 Ibid.

14 Ibid.

15 Jean Baudrillard, *The Transparency of Evil: Essays on Extreme Phenomena*, transl. James Benedict (London: Verso, 1993), p. 189.

16 Jean Baudrillard, *Fatal Strategies*, transl. Phil Beitchman (Los Angeles, CA: Semiotext(e), 1990), p. 129.

17 Ibid., pp. 137f.

Chapter 6. The Aesthetics of Injury

1 Roland Barthes, *A Lover's Discourse: Fragments*, transl. Richard Howard (New York: Hill and Wang, 1978), p. 95.

2 Ibid.

3 Rainer Maria Rilke, *The Notebooks of Malte Laurids Brigge*, trans. Robert Vilain (Oxford: Oxford University Press, 2016), p. 4.

4 Jacques Derrida, 'Que cos' è la poesia?', transl. Peggy Kamuf, in *A Derrida Reader: Between the Blinds* (New York: Harvester/Wheatsheaf, 1991), pp. 222–37; here p. 233.

5 Martin Heidegger, *Parmenides*, transl. André Schuwer and Richard Rojcewicz (Bloomington and Indianapolis, IN: Indiana University Press, 1992), pp. 166f.

6 Roland Barthes, *Camera Lucida*, transl. Richard Howard (New York: Farrar, Straus & Giroux, 1999), p. 27.

7 Cf. ibid., p. 51.

8 Ibid., p. 28.

9 Ibid., p. 27.

10 Ibid., p. 26.

11 Ibid., p. 49. [Transl. note: The second clause is omitted in the English translation.]

12 Ibid., p. 57.

13 Ibid., pp. 57/59.

14 Ibid., p. 41.

15 Ibid., p. 51.

16 Ibid., pp. 51/53.

17 Ibid., p. 41.

18 Ibid., p. 55.

19 Ibid.

20 Ibid.

21 Ibid.

22 Ibid., p. 53.

23 Ibid.

Chapter 7. The Aesthetics of Disaster

1 Immanuel Kant, *Critique of Practical Reason*, transl. Mary Gregor (Cambridge: Cambridge University Press, 2015), p. 129.

2 Georg Wilhelm Friedrich Hegel, *Aesthetics: Lectures on Fine Art*, vol.1, transl. T. M. Knox (Oxford: Clarendon Press, 1975), p. 153.

3 Ibid., p. 154.

4 Ibid., pp. 153f.

5 Maurice Blanchot, *The Writing of the Disaster*, transl. Ann Smock (Lincoln and London: University of Nebraska Press, 1986), p. 120.

6 Ibid., p. 4.

7 Ibid., p. 51.
8 Ibid., p. 133.
9 Ibid., p. 72.
10 Rainer Maria Rilke, *Duino Elegies*, transl. Stephen Mitchell (London: Vintage, 2009), p. 3.
11 Theodor W. Adorno, *Aesthetic Theory*, transl. Robert Hullot-Kentor (London/New York: Continuum, 1997), p. 51.
12 Ibid.
13 Ibid.
14 Ibid.
15 Ibid., p. 52.
16 Ibid., p. 51.
17 Ibid., p. 52.
18 Ibid., p. 73.
19 Ibid., p. 142.
20 Ibid., p. 143.
21 Ibid.
22 Theodor W. Adorno, 'For Anatole France', in *Minima Moralia: Reflections on a Damaged Life*, transl. E. F. N. Jephcott (London and New York: Verso, 2005), pp. 77f.

Chapter 8. The Ideal of Beauty

1 Transl. note: The quotation serves as a motto to the hymn. Hölderlin actually quotes Friedrich Heinrich Jacobi who quotes, with considerable variation, from Kant. See Edward Allwill's Collection of Letters, in *Friedrich Heinrich Jacobi: Main Philosophical Writings and the Novel Allwill*, transl. George de Giovanni, et al. (Montreal: McGill-Queen's University Press, 1994), pp. 379–496; here: p. 385. Jacobi also uses the Kant paraphrase as a motto (see his *Eduard Allwills Briefsammlung*)

(Königsberg: Friedrich Nicolovius, 1792), p. XXVII. The passage in Kant runs: 'It will be said that this explanation of aesthetic judgments in terms of their affinity with moral feeling looks much too studied to be taken as the true interpretation of the cipher by means of which nature figuratively speaks to us in its beautiful forms.' *Critique of the Power of Judgment*, transl. Paul Guyer and Eric Matthews (Cambridge: Cambridge University Press, 2002), p. 180.

2 Kant, *Critique of the Power of Judgment*, p. 120.

3 'Now if in a similar way there is thought for this average man the average head, the average nose, etc., then this shape is the basis for the normal idea of the beautiful man . . .' (ibid., p. 119).

4 Ibid.

5 Ibid.

6 Ibid., fn.

7 Ibid., p. 120.

8 Ibid.

9 Ibid., p. 115.

10 Eva Illouz, *Why Love Hurts: A Sociological Explanation* (Cambridge: Polity, 2012), p. 42.

11 Carl Schmitt, *The Nomos of the Earth (in the International Law of the Jus Publicum Europaeum)*, transl. G. L. Ulmen (New York: Telos Press, 2006), pp. 42f.

12 Carl Schmitt, *Theory of the Partisan*, transl. G. L. Ulmen (New York: Telos Press, 2007), p. 85 (transl. revised; the English translation circumscribes 'Der Feind ist unsere eigene Frage als Gestalt' as 'If the enemy defines us. . .' and adduces an interesting passage from Schmitt's notebooks by way of explanation [see fn. 89, p. 85]. The translation of 'um das eigene Maß, die eigene Grenze, die

eigene Gestalt zu gewinnen' deviates substantially, giving 'in order to be consistent with the definition of the real enemy by which he defines me').

13 Transl. note: 'Friends' in English in the original.

14 Schmitt, *Nomos of the Earth*, p. 42 (transl. mod.).

Chapter 9. Beauty as Truth

1 Georg Wilhelm Friedrich Hegel, *Aesthetics: Lectures on Fine Art*, Vol.1, transl. T. M. Knox (Oxford: Clarendon Press, 1975), p. 116.

2 Ibid., p. 152.

3 Georg Wilhelm Friedrich Hegel, *Elements of the Philosophy of Right*, transl. H. B. Nisbet (Cambridge: Cambridge University Press, 1991), p. 311.

4 Georg Wilhelm Friedrich Hegel, *Hegel's Philosophy of Nature: Part Two of the Encyclopaedia of the Philosophical Sciences (1830)*, transl. A. V. Miller (Oxford: Oxford University Press), p. 300.

5 Georg Wilhelm Friedrich Hegel, *Phenomenology of Spirit*, transl. A. V. Miller (Oxford: Oxford University Press, 1977), p. 277.

6 Hegel, *Aesthetics*, p. 100.

7 Ibid.

8 Ibid., p. 115.

9 Ibid., p. 113 [emphasis on 'subject' restored.

10 Ibid., p. 38.

11 Ibid., p. 114.

12 Ibid.

13 Ibid.

14 Ibid.

15 Ibid.

16 Ibid.

17 Ibid.

18 Georg Wilhelm Friedrich Hegel, *Encyclopaedia of the Philosophical Sciences in Outline, Part 1: Science of Logic*, transl. Klaus Brinkmann and Daniel O. Dahlstrom (Cambridge: Cambridge University Press, 2010), p. 6.

19 Transl. note: See Chris Anderson, 'The End of Theory: The Data Deluge Makes the Scientific Method Obsolete', *Wired*; available at: <https://www.wired.com/2008/06/pb-theory/>.

Chapter 10. The Politics of Beauty

1 Immanuel Kant, *Anthropology from a Pragmatic Point of View*, transl. Robert B. Louden (Cambridge: Cambridge University Press, 2006), pp. 96.

2 Ibid.

3 Hannah Arendt, *The Human Condition* (Chicago, IL, and London: University of Chicago Press, 1958), pp. 12f.

4 Plato, *Republic*, transl. G. M. A. Grube, revsd C. D. C. Reeve (Indianapolis, IN: Hackett, 1997), pp. 971–1223; here p. 999 (358a).

5 'das Schöngute'. The adjectival 'kalos kagathos' is used in the sense of 'the beautiful and good, i.e. perfect, personality'. Hence the noun 'kalokagathia' is usually translated as 'nobility'.

6 'Wahl' also means 'election'.

7 Elaine Scarry, *On Beauty and Being Just* (London: Duckworth, 2000), p. 95.

8 Ibid., p. 109.

9 Ibid., pp. 111f. [Transl. note: The German conflates the two middle sentences into: 'Es ist nicht so, dass wir aufhören, im Zentrum unserer eigenen Welt zu stehen.' = 'It is not that we cease to stand at the center of our

92

own world.', thus inverting the actual meaning. The quotation within the quotation is from Simone Weil, 'Love of the Order of the World', in *Waiting for God* (New York: HarperCollins, 2001), pp. 99–116; here p. 159.]

10 Ibid., p. 114.

11 'Lateralness' and 'centralness', here and below, in English in the original.

Chapter 11. Pornographic Theatre

1 'Am Rande. Wo sonst' [At the margins. Where else], a *Zeit*-conversation with Botho Strauß, in *Die Zeit*, 14 September 2007.

2 'Noch nie einen Menschen von innen gesehen?' [Never seen a human being from the inside?], in *Frankfurter Allgemeine Zeitung*, 17 May 2010.

Chapter 12. Lingering on Beauty

1 Johann Wolfgang Goethe, *Faust: Part I*, trans. David Constantine (London: Penguin, 2005), p. 57 (ls 1699f.).

2 Arthur Schopenhauer, *The World as Will and Representation*, trans. E. F. J. Payne (New York: Dover Publications, 1969), p. 390.

3 Michael Theunissen, *Negative Theologie der Zeit* (Frankfurt/M.: Suhrkamp, 1991), p. 295.

4 Friedrich Nietzsche, *The Gay Science*, trans. Josefine Nauckhoff (Cambridge: Cambridge University Press, 2001), p. 89.

5 Transl. note: 'Hochzeit', literally 'high time', is the German word for 'wedding'. It originally could refer to any festival; within the context of Christianity in particular Easter, Whitsun and Christmas. The German for *Song*

of Solomon, the song of songs, is 'Das Hohelied Salomos' – The High Song of Solomon.

6 Transl. note: The German speaks in the case of both *'Feier'* (celebration) and *'Fest'* (festival) of *'begehen'*: *'ein Fest begehen', 'eine Feier begehen'*.

7 Hans-Georg Gadamer, 'The Relevance of the Beautiful: Art as Play, Symbol and Festival' in *The Relevance of the Beautiful and Other Essays*, trans. Nicholas Walker (Cambridge: Cambridge University Press, 1986), p. 41.

8 Ibid., p. 45.

Chapter 13. Beauty as Reminiscence

1 Walter Benjamin, 'Goethe's Elective Affinities', transl. Stanley Corngold, in *Selected Writings Vol. 1 (1913–1926)* (Cambridge, MA: Harvard University Press, 1996), pp. 297–360; here p. 338.

2 Marcel Proust, *In Search of Lost Time*, vol. 1, 'Swann's Way', transl. C. K. Scott Moncrieff and Terence Kilmartin, revsd D. J. Enright (London: Vintage, 1996), p. 54.

3 Ibid., vol. 6, 'Time Regained', trans. C. K. Scott Moncrieff and Terence Kilmartin, revsd D. J. Enright (London: Vintage, 2000), p. 224.

4 Ibid., p. 245.

5 Ibid., vol. 1, 'Swann's Way', p. 51.

6 Ibid., vol. 6, 'Time Regained', p. 238.

7 Ibid., p. 246.

8 Ibid., p. 222.

9 Ibid., 428.

10 Ibid., p. 246. [The phrase in square brackets is omitted in the English translation.]

11 Friedrich Nietzsche, *Human, All-Too Human*, transl. Marion Faber (London: Penguin, 1994), pp. 104f.

Chapter 14. Giving Birth in Beauty

1 Paul Celan, untitled poem, in *Selected Poems*, transl. Michael Hamburger (London: Penguin, 1996), p. 271.
2 Plato, *Symposium*, transl. Alexander Nehamas and Paul Woodruff, in *Complete Works* (Indianapolis, IN: Hackett, 1997), p. 489 (206b).
3 Martin Heidegger, Letter of 14 February 1950, in *Letters to His Wife (1915–1970)*, transl. R. D. V. Glasgow (Polity: Cambridge, 2008), p. 213.
4 Martin Heidegger, *Zu Hölderlin. Griechenlandreisen* [On Hölderlin. Journeys to Greece], *Gesamtausgabe*, vol. 75 (Frankfurt/M.: Klostermann, 2000), p. 29.
5 Martin Heidegger, *The Essence of Truth: On Plato's Cave Allegory and Theaetetus*, transl. Ted Sadler (London and New York: Continuum, 2002), p. 170.
6 Martin Heidegger, 'The Origin of the Work of Art', in *Off the Beaten Track*, transl. Julian Young and Kenneth Haynes (Cambridge: Cambridge University Press, 2002), p. 52 (trans. mod.).
7 Plato, *Symposium*, p. 493 (211b).
8 Ibid., 211a.
9 Alain Badiou (in conversation with Nicolas Truong), *In Praise of Love*, trans. Peter Bush (London: Serpent's Tail, 2012), p. 44.